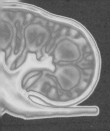
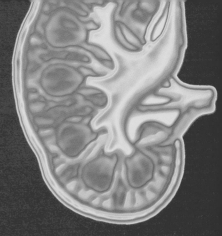

Medical Imaging

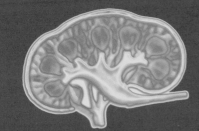

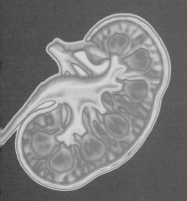

GREAT INVENTIONS

Medical Imaging

VICTORIA SHERROW

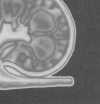

Marshall Cavendish
Benchmark
New York

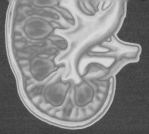
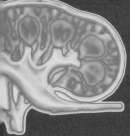

Marshall Cavendish Benchmark
99 White Plains Road
Tarrytown, NY 10591-9001
www.marshallcavendish.us

Library of Congress Cataloging-in-Publication Data

Sherrow, Victoria.
Medical imaging / by Victoria Sherrow.
p. cm. — (Great inventions)
Summary: "An examination of the origins, history, development, and societal impact of various medical-imaging devices, from x-rays to MRIs"—Provided by publisher.
Includes bibliographical references and index.
ISBN-13: 978-0-7614-2231-0
ISBN-10: 0-7614-2231-5
1. Diagnostic imaging—Juvenile literature.   I. Title. II. Series.
RC78.7.D53S44 2007
616.07'54—dc22

2006003229

Series design by Sonia Chaghatzbanian

Photo research by Candlepants Incorporated

Cover photo: Corbis

The photographs in this book are used by permission and through the courtesy of:
Corbis: Andrew Brookes, 2; Bernardo Bucci, 8; Bettmann, 16, 26, 29, 38, 89; Hulton-Deutsch, 34; Hulton Deutsch Collection, 36; Firefly Productions, 45, 73; Lester Lefkowitz, 48, 61, 62, 79, 80; Jim Craigmyle, 50; Roger Ressmeyer, 91; Howard Sochurek, 97. *Photo Researchers Inc.*: Phanie, 11, 70; Biophoto Associates, 12; SPL, 22; Science Photo Library, 24; J.L. Charmet, 28; Neil Borden, 41; Petit Format, 54; Saturn Stills, 57; A.Pasieka, 67; Zephyr, 76; Mary Evans, 83; Jim Dowdalls, 93; Mike Agliolo, 94; Roger Harris, 99. *The Image Works*: SSPL, 14, 15, 19, 27; Lebrecht Music & Arts, 85.

Printed in China
1 3 5 6 4 2

CONTENTS

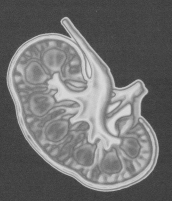

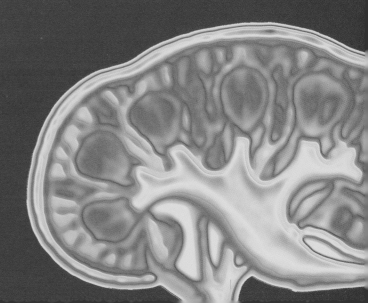

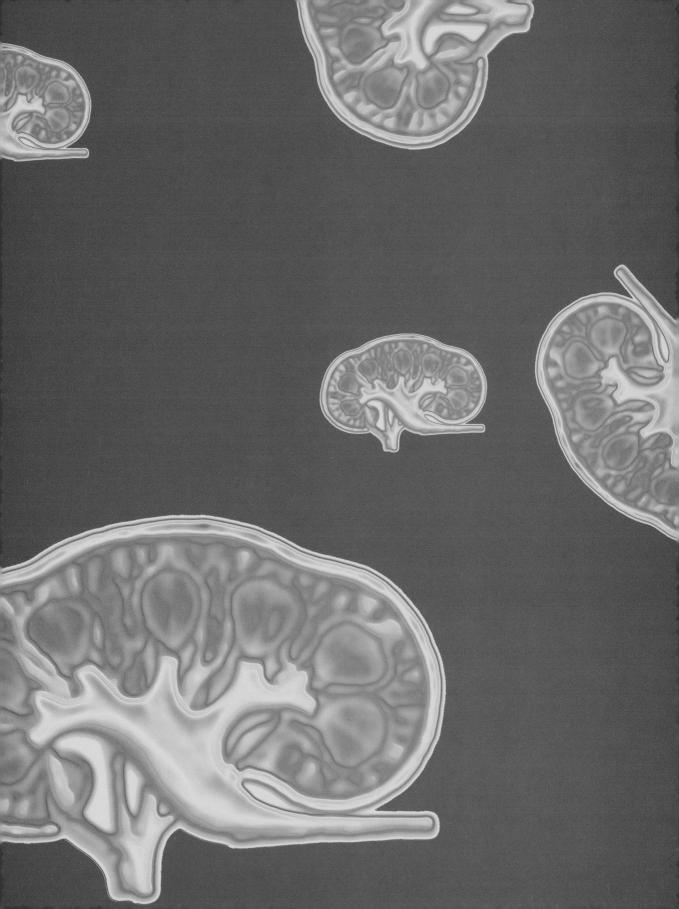

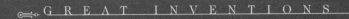

Medical Imaging

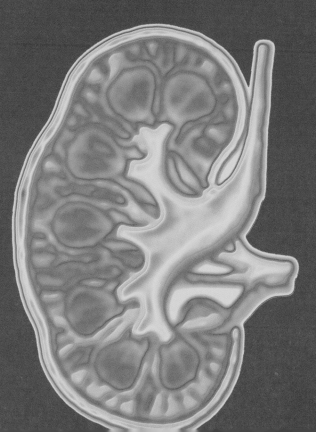

OFTEN IN AN EMERGENCY ROOM SETTING, THE DEATH OF A PATIENT IS IMMINENT, AND THE RIGHT DECISION IS KEY. DOCTORS AND OTHER HEALTH PROFESSIONALS NEED ACCURATE INFORMATION AS FAST AS POSSIBLE, IN ORDER TO DETERMINE THE BEST COURSE OF ACTION.

"A New Kind of Light"

Every day people arrive at clinics or emergency rooms (ERs) seeking treatment for a variety of injuries and illnesses. Patients visit health care professionals for check-ups or to receive help for specific problems. Sometimes young people need emergency care after a bad fall or an unexpected accident or complication. Accident victims may experience pain, along with swelling and bruises. They may have torn ligaments or tendons or suffer a cracked or broken bone.

A correct diagnosis is needed in order to plan the best treatment. If no bones are broken, the doctor may order a cold pack and prescribe rest and medication to reduce pain and inflammation. But a fracture requires other treatments, including a cast designed to keep the broken edges of the bone in place while the injury heals. If the bone is broken in several places, surgeons may need to wire the pieces of bone together before a cast can be applied.

During an exam, doctors observe and touch a patient's injured limb and ask questions. But they cannot see through the skin to the bones inside, so they often order an x-ray or other form of diagnostic imaging. The patient is then taken to the x-ray area and carefully positioned. The body part being x-rayed is placed close to a cassette containing film. Then, while the patient remains still, a beam is focused on the area. The exposure usually lasts less than one second, and soon thereafter, the doctor can see an image of the patient's bones.

Before 1896 doctors had to rely on their own experience and judgment as well as guesswork when diagnosing injuries or diseases they could not see. There was a great margin for error. Incorrect or inaccurate conclusions and diagnoses could lead to serious problems. Sometimes a doctor felt compelled to perform exploratory surgery, which was invasive, time consuming, and frequently risky for the patient. With the onset of x-ray technology, medical professionals suddenly had a way to "image" an injury. This turning point in medical history marked the beginning of what some people now call "the age of medical imaging."

Today, health care practitioners can examine bones and internal organs, even tiny ducts and blood vessels, using modern x-rays and other techniques that scan the body. These procedures are considered safe when performed by qualified personnel using the proper equipment. They are also relatively painless and convenient because they are non-invasive—that is, they do not require cutting into or entering the body. Modern technology can produce sharp, detailed images that provide clear distinctions among neighboring tissues. As an added benefit, the information is available fairly quickly, sometimes during the test itself.

Through the years, medical imaging has become increasingly common, with more than a quarter billion imaging procedures performed annually in the United States alone. A typical medical-imaging center or imaging department in a hospital or medical office performs a variety of procedures ranging from simple x-rays to complicated computer-assisted tests. People working in this specific field, called radiology, include physicians, nurses, technologists, and technicians. They have special training in taking, analyzing, and interpreting medical images.

X-raying and computer-assisted imaging are done not only for diagnostic purposes but for preventive reasons as well—to detect problems and diseases earlier. Examples of preventive tests are those that measure bone density in people at risk for osteoporosis (the loss of bone mass) and mammograms to check breast tissue for cancerous tumors. Dentists and orthodontists also rely on x-rays to help them treat their patients and detect problems.

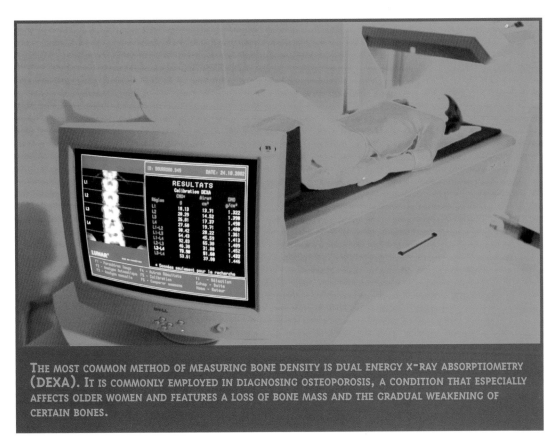

THE MOST COMMON METHOD OF MEASURING BONE DENSITY IS DUAL ENERGY X-RAY ABSORPTIOMETRY (DEXA). IT IS COMMONLY EMPLOYED IN DIAGNOSING OSTEOPOROSIS, A CONDITION THAT ESPECIALLY AFFECTS OLDER WOMEN AND FEATURES A LOSS OF BONE MASS AND THE GRADUAL WEAKENING OF CERTAIN BONES.

X-rays have been most useful in cases in which a disease or disorder has changed the structure of the body in some way—such as a broken bone. X-rays can show abnormal curvature in the spine and certain diseases in the joints. The images also reveal the buildup of fluid in the lung and some lung diseases, including pneumonia, cancer, and asbestosis—a disease in which long-term exposure to asbestos damages the lung tissue. Scar tissue from asbestosis shows up in x-ray films in the form of abnormal shadows. A patient who complains of shortness of breath even while resting might be given a chest x-ray to check for this and other lung-related ailments.

While x-rays gave people their first look inside the living body, CT (computed tomography) scanning and MRIs (magnetic resonance imaging) provide cross-sectional images and show subtle conditions that are not apparent or detectable with x-rays. Nuclear medicine, ultrasonography, and other kinds of medical imaging provide still more options for

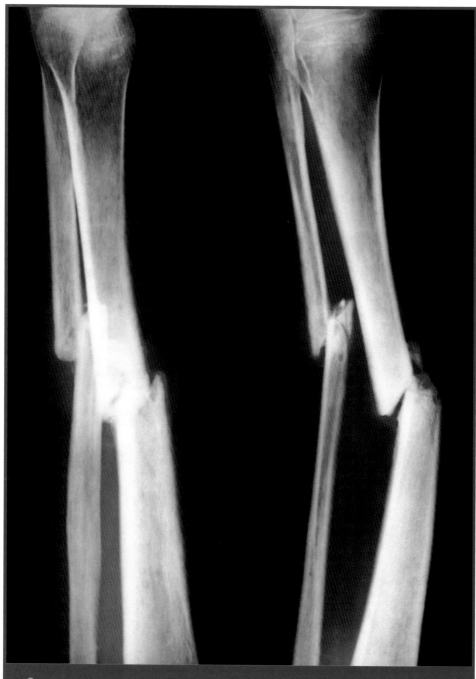

ONE OF THE MOST COMMON APPLICATIONS OF X-RAYS IS THE DETECTION OF BROKEN BONES. THIS COLOR-ENHANCED X-RAY SHOWS A FRACTURED TIBIA AND FIBULA. THE TIBIA, ANOTHER NAME FOR THE SHINBONE, SUPPORTS THE BODY'S WEIGHT, WHILE THE FIBULA, A SMALLER BONE, RUNS ALONGSIDE THE TIBIA BELOW THE KNEE.

diagnosing illnesses and assessing a person's state of health. The methods of medical imaging rely on different tools and technology, but they do all share a common goal: tracking a certain area and recording what they find there. In each method, a kind of exploratory "probe," usually a form of energy, is passed through the body. This probe passes through some areas better than others, and that process produces data that can be assembled into images showing tissues in the body. With ultrasonography, the sound waves do not pass through the body completely but are reflected, and the echoes then recorded.

The first type of medical imaging, x-rays, surfaced in an era that featured major advances in science and technology. Scientists and inventors were finding new ways to capture sights and sounds and use them in practical ways. The telephone came into use in 1876, followed by the phonograph the next year. Photography was advancing, too, and cameras for non-professionals became available during the 1880s. In December 1895, French brothers Auguste and Louis Lumiere used a new kind of camera they built to project the world's first motion picture before an audience. Their brief film of a moving locomotive was just a hint of the advances to come.

Like many great achievements, the discovery of x-rays built on the work of numerous people. During the 1800s, scientists in various countries were studying electricity, magnetism, and radioactivity. They often used a device called a vacuum tube for their experiments. The first practical vacuum tube came from German Johann Heinrich Wilhelm Geissler (1815–1879), the son of a glassmaker. In the mid-1850s, Geissler invented an effective vacuum pump as well as a method for sealing metal electrodes inside a glass tube. When he connected the electrodes to a source of electricity, a soft light glowed inside the tube. Geissler added different gases to the tubes and observed a similar glow being emitted. The colors varied, depending on the gas. Still, despite the vacuum pump, a slight amount of air remained inside the Geissler tube.

WILLIAM CROOKES IN A PHOTOGRAPH TAKEN AROUND 1850. THE SHREWD CHEMIST AND PHYSICIST MADE CONTRIBUTIONS TO SEVERAL SCIENTIFIC FIELDS. HE INVENTED THE RADIOMETER, A DEVICE THAT RESPONDS TO LIGHT AND OTHER ELECTROMAGNETIC RADIATION. HE DEVELOPED THE FIRST SPINTHARISCOPE, WHICH MADE ALPHA PARTICLES VISIBLE; DISCOVERED THE ELEMENT THALLIUM; AND WAS AN AGRICULTURE AND SANITATION EXPERT AS WELL.

A British scientist, William Crookes, improved on the invention, devising a vacuum pump that could remove the air from the tube. With the air gone, the tube no longer lit up and faint rays came from the negative electrode. As these rays hit the glass of the tube, they created a luminous greenish gold area. This device became subsequently known as the Crookes tube.

Crookes described the "radiant matter" and "molecular rays" he observed during his experiments. At the time, physicists called these streams of negatively charged particles cathode rays. Today they are called electrons. In Crookes's tube, electrons were released from the surface of a metal plate, called the cathode, fixed in a vacuum within a glass tube.

Hungarian physicist Philipp Lenard developed a new version of the Crookes tube by placing a thin plate of aluminum in the glass wall. When rays struck the metal plate, they penetrated to the depth of about 1 inch (2.5 centimeters). Lenard demonstrated this phenomenon in a darkened lab. He coated a piece of cardboard with a phosphorescent chemical and held it close to the aluminum plate. It gave off a faint glow. Lenard was able to intensify this glow by covering the whole tube, except for the plate, with black paper.

Physicist Wilhelm Conrad Roentgen (1845–1923) then added a new development to the work of this chain of pioneers. He was using

Lenard's version of the Crookes tube to study light phenomena when he accidentally encountered x-rays. Roentgen, a German-born Dutch citizen, had studied at the Utrecht Technical School in the Netherlands and at the Zurich Polytechnic School in Switzerland. In 1888 he was

made a professor at the University of Wurzburg in Germany and took charge of their new physics institute. Like many others, Roentgen was interested in cathode rays. He had conducted experiments in which a high voltage was applied between two wires sealed in a glass Crookes tube, causing a fluorescent glow to appear.

In the late afternoon on November 8, 1895, Roentgen was again experimenting with the flow of electricity through a vacuum tube. He had speculated that cathode rays might penetrate the glass wall of the Crookes tube if he used an intense electrical current. Roentgen wrapped black cardboard around the vacuum tube to prevent any light from escaping from it. He then turned off the lights in the lab and switched on the current inside his tube.

WILHELM CONRAD ROENTGEN WAS ORIGINALLY AN ENGINEERING STUDENT IN ZURICH BEFORE TURNING TO PHYSICS AND LATER TEACHING THE SUBJECT AT THE UNIVERSITY OF WURZBURG. HIS PIONEERING RESEARCH WITH CATHODE RAYS AND HIS DISCOVERY OF X-RAYS PAVED THE WAY TO RECEIVING THE FIRST NOBEL PRIZE IN PHYSICS, AWARDED IN 1901.

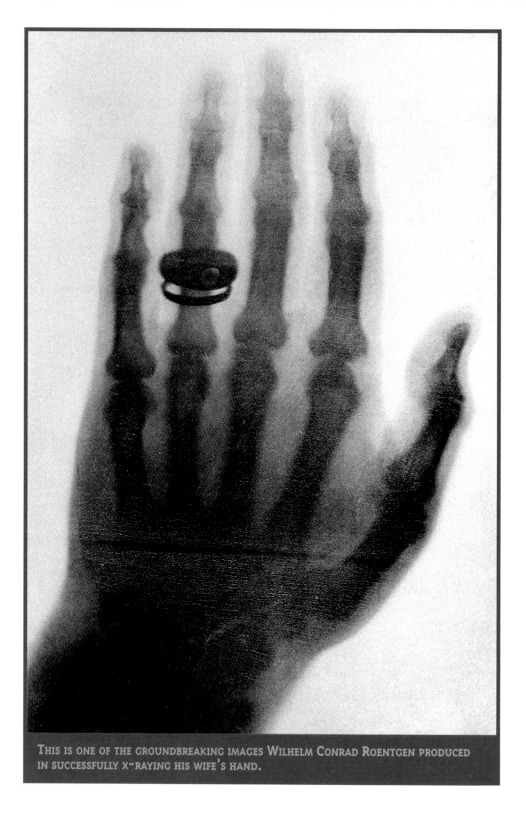

THIS IS ONE OF THE GROUNDBREAKING IMAGES WILHELM CONRAD ROENTGEN PRODUCED IN SUCCESSFULLY X-RAYING HIS WIFE'S HAND.

16

To his surprise, a faint light glowed from an object on his workbench, located about 4 feet (1.2 meters) away from the tube. Roentgen lit a match so that he could investigate further. The light came from a small cardboard screen coated with barium platinocyanide, a phosphorescent chemical that was used in those days to develop photographic plates. When he switched the current on and off in the tube, the glow on the screen appeared and disappeared accordingly. When he moved the screen farther away, the light still glowed.

Roentgen concluded that the rays coming from his vacuum tube were more powerful than mere cathode rays. He set out to investigate these mysterious rays that could penetrate both air and the light-proof black cardboard surrounding his tube. For nearly two months, Roentgen worked alone without discussing his findings. He discovered that the rays could penetrate other objects, including wood, rubber, a thousand-page book, and different metals. The rays moved through some substances more easily than others, but could not penetrate lead. When Roentgen held a piece of lead between his tube and the fluorescent screen, he saw the shadow of the lead on the screen. He also saw the clear outline of his fingers and the larger bones in his hand. The rays apparently could not penetrate bone, either.

To explore this phenomenon further, Roentgen asked his wife, Bertha, to hold her hand on a photographic plate while he directed the rays at it for fifteen minutes. When he developed the plate, it showed a clear outline of her hand and the bones inside, along with the two rings on her finger. Not only did the rays cause fluorescence and penetrate certain materials, they could be used to produce an image on a photographic plate.

But what were these mysterious rays? Roentgen did not know, so he called the phenomenon X radiation or x-rays. The *X* referred to something unknown, as it does in mathematics. Other scientists, including Crookes and Lenard, had observed this same phenomenon but did not grasp what was happening. In fact, more than a century earlier, a Welsh mathematician named William Morgan also knew of these rays. He was working with electrical discharges in a vacuum when he noticed that boiling mercury produced an unusual light. Unlike Roentgen, who was color-blind, Morgan could see the glow's changing colors. He wrote that "the 'electric' light turned violet, then purple, then a beautiful green . . . and then the light became invisible."

On December 28, Roentgen published his findings in a journal, spurring other scientists to pose questions about the nature of the discovery. Since then, experts have determined that x-rays are a form of invisible electromagnetic radiation having a short wavelength. They are part of the electromagnetic spectrum, which also includes ultraviolet light waves, visible light waves, microwaves, and radio waves. X-rays result when high-energy electrons hit the atoms of a material object. This impact releases a stream of small particles called photons. The photons in x-rays are more energized than those in visible light. Their energy depends on the intensity of the power source that produces the electrons. X-rays are more penetrating than ultraviolet light and have a range of wavelengths, measuring from .01 to 10 nanometers—between .01 and 10 one billionths of a meter or, put another way, between .01 and 10 1/1,000,000,000 of a centimeter. The wavelengths of the rays are much shorter than the wavelengths of visible light, which measure between 4,000 and 7,000 Angstroms. (An Angstrom equals 0.1 nanometers or .0000000001 meters). Inside a vacuum, the speed of x-rays is the same as visible light.

After Roentgen's article appeared, professional journals around the world spread the news. The popular press also picked up the story. Headlines such as NEW LIGHT SEES THROUGH FLESH AND BONES! attracted plenty of attention. Some articles included photographs showing foot bones seen through shoes or the coins inside a woman's purse. In an era when people praised modesty and clothing hid most of the body, many people were

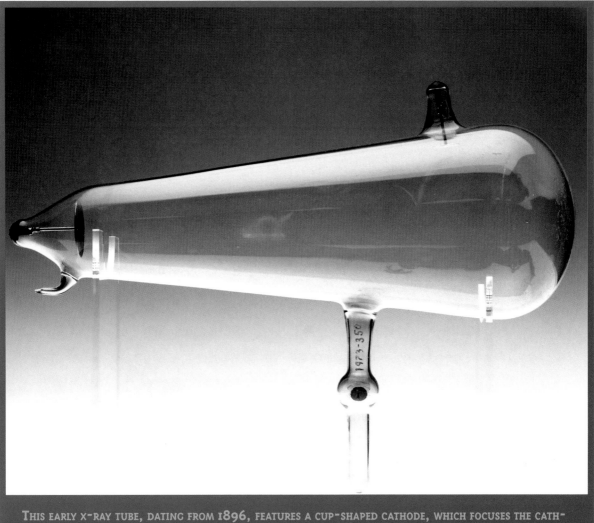

THIS EARLY X-RAY TUBE, DATING FROM 1896, FEATURES A CUP-SHAPED CATHODE, WHICH FOCUSES THE CATHODES RAYS ONTO THE TARGETED AREA, IN THIS CASE A PLATINUM ANODE. WHEN THE RAYS STRIKE THE ANODE, THE ENERGY THEY CONTAIN IS TRANSFORMED INTO X-RAYS, WHICH THEN PASS OUT THROUGH THE GLASS.

shocked by the idea of a scientific device that could "see" through their garments.

In some circles the concern grew, and rumors spread that these new rays could be used for strange, even sinister, purposes. One story described "x-ray eyeglasses" that let people see through other people or view their naked bodies through clothing. As a result, a company in London began selling "x-ray proof underwear." A farmer from Iowa claimed that x-rays could be used to transform other metals into gold. Writers developed storylines involving x-rays, and cartoonists also mined this new discovery. Some editorials speculated that x-ray machines would become standard equipment in people's homes. Meanwhile, curious people paid photographers called skiagraphers for "bone portraits." They put coins into commercial fluoroscopy machines that let them see the bones in their hands or feet.

As for practical applications, some people foresaw industrial uses, such as checking metal bridges for cracks not visible to the human eye. More importantly, people saw how x-rays could benefit medical practice. They allowed doctors to look inside the body to obtain important information. The ability to see organs and structures inside a living body meant that physicians could forego certain exploratory procedures that were performed just to find out what was wrong. X-ray imaging reduced some of the guesswork involved in medical diagnosis and treatment, particularly when it came to diseases or injuries involving bones. Bones are denser than the surrounding tissues, which include skin, muscle, and fat. X-rays pass through these less dense tissues but are blocked by the calcium in bones. The rays then blacken photographic film, leaving the shadow of bone as a white area. The soft tissues around bones appear on film in shades of gray.

X-rays ushered in a new era of more accurate diagnosis and improved procedures. This new technology also raised serious questions and issues. It was the first medical technique that did not involve direct contact between doctor and patient. How would this new distance change the nature of the traditional doctor-patient relationship? Who would use x-ray machines and interpret the resulting images? What kind of training and credentials would these people need? As time went on, people also expressed their increasing concerns over safety as they looked for ways to protect patients and health care workers from the harmful effects of radiation.

By 1896 x-ray machines had been installed in several London hospitals. The patient was required to stay still for significant periods of time. Due to a lack of understanding of the dangerous effects of x-rays, early operators were exposed to harmful levels of radiation.

Developments and Dilemmas

Within weeks after Roentgen's article first appeared, doctors in Europe and the United States were using x-rays. Companies started selling x-ray equipment while some individuals, particularly physicists working in university labs, tried making their own. By the end of 1896, physicians and hospitals in many cities and even small towns had acquired an x-ray machine.

The first diagnostic radiograph in America has been credited to Edwin Frost, an astronomy professor at Dartmouth College. On February 3, 1896, Frost and his brother, a physician, x-rayed the forearm of a fourteen-year-old boy to examine a broken bone. They used vacuum tubes from the college's physics laboratory. An account of this historic event appeared in the winter 1995 issue of *Dartmouth Medicine*. It includes a quote from Edwin Frost that appeared in *Science* magazine two weeks after the x-ray was taken: "It was possible yesterday to test the method upon a broken arm. After an exposure of 20 minutes the plate on development showed the fracture in the ulna very distinctively." Frost also predicted "numerous applications of the new method in the sciences and arts . . ."

Broken bones were one of the obvious "applications" Frost envisioned. Additional uses soon emerged. X-rays could help doctors locate foreign objects in the body, including a broken sewing needle lodged in a woman's wrist. In February 1896, in Rochester, Minnesota, Doctor J. G. Cross used his new x-ray machine to find a belt buckle a young child had swallowed. The outline showed how the prongs were positioned, which helped the surgeon remove it safely. Doctors also used x-rays to study malformed spines and other congenital (inborn) abnormalities in infants and children. Physicians could see the stones that formed inside the gall bladder and the kidneys, causing painful symptoms and disease. A rhyme from those days—"bullets, bones, and kidney stones"—describes three common medical uses for x-rays and the objects they detected.

As the demand increased, doctors who lacked access to x-ray equipment often referred patients to other physicians, to a commercial x-ray lab, or to a university physics lab that could do the procedure. People founded x-ray businesses to make and sell equipment, as well as to generate the x-rays themselves. These businesses advertised their services in medical journals as well as in mainstream media outlets. Some labs were located in the homes of their operators. Others became large commercial enterprises. In Chicago, for example, the Schmidt-Harnisch laboratory was run by an electrical engineer named Wolfram C. Fuchs. He had visited Germany shortly after Roentgen published his findings and decided to pursue this new field. Fuchs's radiographs were admired for their clarity, and physicians respected his skills. In 1896 the lab performed more than 1,400 x-ray exams. Fuchs may have been one of the first people to radiograph kidney stones, gallstones, the hip joint, and an aortic aneurysm.

The military also embraced x-ray technology since it could be used to find bullets lodged in people's bodies as well as diagnose other kinds of

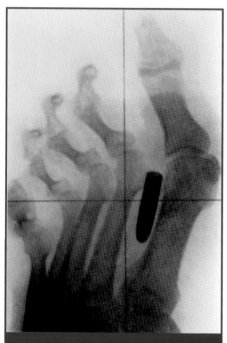

EARLY X-RAY TECHNOLOGY PROVED EFFECTIVE IN WARTIME, ALLOWING DOCTORS TO TREAT SOME WOUNDED SOLDIERS MORE EFFECTIVELY. THIS X-RAY SHOWS A MAUSER BULLET LODGED BETWEEN THE METATARSAL BONES OF THE BIG AND SECOND TOES OF A MAN WHO SERVED IN THE BOER WAR, FOUGHT BETWEEN THE BRITISH AND THE DUTCH SETTLERS OF SOUTH AFRICA. TO MAKE THE RADIOGRAPH, THE SOLDIER POSITIONED HIS FOOT ABOVE A PHOTOGRAPHIC PLATE, WHICH WAS THEN BOMBARDED WITH X-RAYS FROM AN OPEN ELECTRIC DISCHARGE TUBE.

injuries soldiers suffered in combat. In 1898, the British military took mobile x-ray units to Sudan, where soldiers were fighting against the people called the Mahdi or the Mahdists. During the Spanish-American War, which occurred that same year, U.S. military doctors used x-rays in hospitals, and x-ray machines were placed on board four American military ships.

Dr. Henry W. Cattell echoed the thoughts of many others when he wrote that "the manifold uses to which Roentgen's discovery may be applied in medicine are so obvious that it is even now questionable whether a surgeon would be morally justified in performing a certain class of operations without first having seen pictured by these rays the field of his work." Cattell called x-rays "a map . . . of the unknown country he is to explore."

Dentists began using x-rays in 1896, too. Teeth are even denser than bone, and x-rays can show teeth located inside the gum, as well as those above the surface. Dr. William Morton of New York City was one of the first people to perform dental radiography in the United States. He also wrote a book called *The X-ray,* published in 1896. Soon, dental histories became a key part of forensic medicine—the use of medical information to solve crimes. Police used dental records to identify a body in France in 1897.

Meanwhile, scientists sought to improve the quality of x-ray images, making them clearer, more detailed, and more accurate. Practitioners also wanted to view a greater number of organs and areas inside the body. New technology based on physics, chemistry, and photography aided this pursuit. One big step forward was the focus tube, which was introduced in March 1896. Its creator, Englishman Major Herbert Jackson, used a curved cathode plate so that rays were focused in a line as they struck the opposing anode plate. The rays were more contained and unified as they reached their target, an adjustment that helped prevent the blurring that resulted when random rays hit the plate. Focus tubes also made it possible to complete x-rays faster, which meant there was less movement in the patient, less exposure to radiation, and a

ANOTHER EARLY TYPE OF X-RAY MACHINE. IN THE LATE 1890S AND EARLY YEARS OF THE TWENTIETH CENTURY, WITH THE PROCEDURE STILL IN ITS INFANCY, X-RAY TECHNIQUE WAS REFINED AND GRADUALLY IMPROVED.

sharper image was produced as well. Despite the advances, many operators continued to hold sessions lasting an hour or more.

Another improvement came from the American inventor and electrical pioneer Elihu Thomson. His stereo x-ray camera could be positioned in a more precise manner than previous units. Thomas Edison, the renowned inventor of the lightbulb and the phonograph, worked to improve other aspects of x-ray technology. He also tried, unsuccessfully, to capture images of the brain. Scientists and laypeople alike were curious to see a live human brain. One of the most notorious x-ray frauds occurred in 1896 when photographer H. A. Falk sold a newspaper an image that he claimed was an x-ray of a living human brain. It was later revealed to be a picture of cat intestines arranged in the shape of a brain.

Despite the actions of con men, scientific knowledge relating to x-rays continued to advance. An historic discovery took place in 1897 when British physicist J. J. Thomson showed that cathode rays were

ANOTHER EARLY WINNER OF THE NOBEL PRIZE FOR PHYSICS, J. J. THOMPSON MADE HIS NAME INITIALLY EXPERIMENTING WITH CATHODE RAYS. HIS RESEARCH HELPED SETTLE A RAGING DEBATE. BRITISH PHYSICISTS ARGUED THAT CATHODE RAYS WERE PARTICLES, WHILE GERMAN SCIENTISTS MAINTAINED THAT THE RAYS WERE ACTUALLY A FORM OF ELECTROMAGNETIC RADIATION. THOMSON SETTLED THE MATTER BY SHOWING THAT CATHODE RAYS WERE NEGATIVELY CHARGED PARTICLES SMALLER THAN ATOMS IN SIZE.

negatively charged particles. Thomson was surprised to find that these particles, which he called "small bodies," were smaller than an atom with a mass 1,800 times less than hydrogen, the lightest element. Thomson's work disproved the long-held theories that atoms were the smallest particles found in nature and that they were indivisible. His research also helped to explain the nature of Roentgen's "mysterious rays," the charged particles in the cathode rays now known as electrons. An additional discovery followed in 1912 when German physicist Max von Laue showed that x-rays are a form of electromagnetic radiation.

Roentgen remained famous as "the man who discovered x-rays," but he never obtained any patents and chose not to profit from his research. In 1901 he received the first Nobel Prize given for physics. Roentgen donated the money that comes with the award to scientific work at his university. He also promoted the name *x-rays* and urged people not to call them "Roentgen rays."

In the early 1900s the use of x-rays increased, as doctors and hospital administrators increasingly saw their application and value to the practice of medicine. Their use during wartime strongly influenced this process. The British led the way by using x-rays both in their permanent military facilities and in field hospitals where machines were battery powered. During World War I (1914–1918), more and more people had x-rays or saw the process being administered.

Doctors quickly recognized that x-rays were useful for diagnosing tuberculosis (TB), an infectious lung disease that was prevalent at the turn of the century. During World War I, as

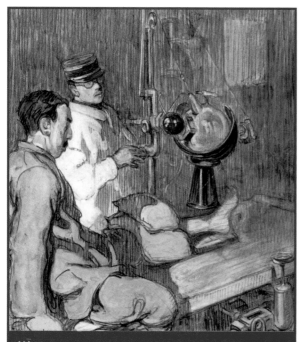

WAR AGAIN PROVIDED NUMEROUS PRACTICAL APPLICATIONS OF THE EVOLVING X-RAY TECHNOLOGY. THIS PAINTING SHOWS X-RAY EQUIPMENT IN USE DURING WORLD WAR I.

doctors performed chest x-rays on troops and veterans, they noticed variations in their lungs and saw dark areas in the lungs of men who smoked. Some men had tubercular scars and active cases of TB that had not been detected during a physical exam. Using x-ray imaging was thus a breakthrough in diagnosing a serious disease, although there was then no cure for TB. This particular dilemma would persist into the twenty-first century as science made it possible to diagnose medical conditions that could not yet be cured. Patients suffering from TB were told to eat healthy foods, rest, and avoid infecting others.

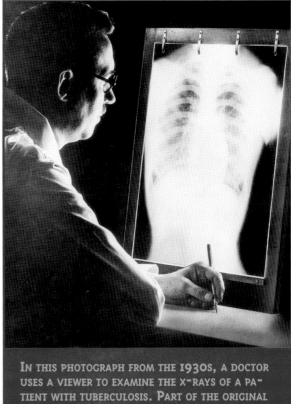

IN THIS PHOTOGRAPH FROM THE 1930S, A DOCTOR USES A VIEWER TO EXAMINE THE X-RAYS OF A PATIENT WITH TUBERCULOSIS. PART OF THE ORIGINAL CAPTION READ, "THE X-RAY IS THE DETECTIVE THAT PUTS THE FINGER ON THE DEADLY MASQUERADER NO MATTER WHAT DISGUISE IT WORE IN GETTING INTO THE BODY." TUBERCULOSIS WAS A SERIOUS AND THREATENING CONCERN.

After World War I, more hospitals bought x-ray machines so they could perform "medical roentgenography" on site. Hospitals that could not afford new equipment bought used machines. Administrators looked for physicians with special training in electricity or photography to operate the equipment. The x-ray departments in large hospitals took thousands of x-rays each year. These labs were usually located in the hospital basement, and many were poorly designed and even hazardous. Still, doctors at more advanced facilities were glad they did not have to send patients elsewhere.

As a result of the growing embrace of x-ray technology, radiology developed as a profession, with a specific body of knowledge and special organizations and journals for its practitioners. In France, Antoine Béclère, known as the "father of French Roentgenography," helped to found and develop a laboratory at the Hospital Ténon. Béclère worked in one small room with no assistants, so his wife helped him to develop the films at home. He had left his previous field, immunology, to study x-rays and their medical uses. Antoine Béclère is thought to have coined the term *radiologie*—in English, "radiology"—for this new medical specialty.

The year 1896 also saw the publication of the first textbook on the subject: *Practical Radiography* by H. Snowden Ward. British physicians organized the Roentgen Society and founded a journal called *Archives of the Röntgen Ray,* adopting a variation of the pioneer's name. In London, the *Archives of Clinical Skiagraphy,* which also debuted in 1896, was the first widely read journal about radiology. Its name eventually changed to *Archives of the Roentgen Ray,* it included articles and photographs by respected physicians, which helped to boost the reputation of this new field. As knowledge grew, more textbooks appeared. Two of the most widely used were *The Practical Application of the Röntgen Rays in Therapeutics and Diagnosis,* by W. A. Pusey and E. W. Caldwell (1903) and *Röntgen Rays and Electro-therapeutics* by Mihran Kassabian (1907).

Schools were set up to train radiologists, and medical schools added radiology classes to the curriculum. Laypeople, including photographers and electricians, took nonmedical correspondence courses that, on completion, offered the title doctor of roentgenology. Some radiology pioneers were self-taught or came from other professions. A number of them had once assisted doctors who performed x-rays. William Dodd began as a janitor before working his way up in the radiology field. Dodd later established the radiology department at Massachusetts General Hospital and was appointed as its first roentgenologist.

Heber Robarts, a physician practicing in Saint Louis, Missouri, founded the American Roentgen Ray Society in 1900. Members, who paid five dollars annually in dues, received the *American X-ray Journal.* It contained news about their profession and articles about radiological practices in different facilities throughout the country. Robarts also founded the Saint Louis Ray Laboratory, which offered classes for physicians.

A 1901 textbook called *The Roentgen Rays in Medicine and*

Surgery was written by Francis Williams, a physician who became known as the "first American radiologist." The x-ray lab that he organized with his brother-in-law Dr. William Rollins at Boston City Hospital was advanced for its time. Along with equipment, it featured a dressing room, an examination room, and a darkroom for developing photographic plates. More importantly, Williams and Rollins improved the existing equipment and added safety features to protect people from potentially harmful radiation. The cathode tube was placed inside a box Rollins had developed, made from materials that x-rays could not penetrate.

Women were also among the radiology pioneers. San Francisco resident Elizabeth Fleischmann began studying x-ray work in 1896. After taking a six-month course in electrical science, she set up her own x-ray office, one of the first in California and quickly gained the respect of her peers. Photographs of her work appeared in journals and in U.S. Army publications relating to the medical use of x-rays on soldiers fighting in the Spanish-American War. Fleischmann was one of the forty-two founding members of the Roentgen Society of the United States. Her profession led to radiation-induced cancer, however. In 1903 Fleischmann developed what people called x-ray dermatitis on her hands. The next year, her right arm and shoulder were amputated. She died in 1905. Another pioneer, May Cushman Rice, a physician, taught x-ray therapy and diagnosis in Illinois. She was most likely the first woman to teach radiographic technique in the United States.

In 1902, Irish-born Florence Ada Stoney, a graduate of the London School of Medicine for Women, started the x-ray department at London's Royal Free Hospital. Because of her gender, the British War Department refused Stoney's offer to serve as a radiologist during World War I. So she headed the medical staff and radiology unit of a women's volunteer unit. This unit received a star for bravery in 1914, and Stoney was appointed head of the x-ray department of Fulham military hospital in 1915. This made her the first woman the War Department had ever hired for a full-time position.

Overall, people working in radiology continued to organize and promote their profession. In 1920 Ed Jerman of Chicago founded the American Association of Radiological Technicians (later the American Society of X-ray Technicians). Formed in 1923 as an honorary group for physicians who practiced radiology, the American College of Radiology later took on a more active political role. In 1939 the American Roentgen Ray Society, Radiological Society of North America, and American Radium Society began working together to promote their common interests.

By then, radiologists had better equipment. In 1913 Gustav Bucky had found a new way to reduce the scattering of rays, which caused blurry images. He inserted a metal grid between the patient and the x-ray tube and another grid between the patient and the photographic plate. After Hollis E. Potter refined and improved the grids to make them movable, they became known as Bucky-Potter grids.

That same year, American physicist William David Coolidge developed an improved x-ray tube. He was trying to find better filament materials for electric lightbulbs when he decided to replace the platinum anode in the x-ray tube with tungsten, after he found a way to make the metal less brittle. Working with Irving Langmuir, he was able to remove nearly all the gas from the tube, which made it more powerful. Unlike earlier tubes, the cathode in Coolidge's tube was heated by an auxiliary current instead of by ions. High voltage sent across the tube then accelerated the electrons that came from the heated cathode. Increasing voltage produces a decrease in the minimum wavelength of the radiation. The resulting radiation became easier to control, less scattered, and more reliable from one image to another. Most of today's x-ray tubes are modified versions of Coolidge's innovation. The larger, more powerful modern x-ray tubes feature water-cooled anticathodes (anodes), which prevent melting due to the electron bombardment in the tube.

Although x-rays were a boon to medicine, they posed unforeseen dangers to patients and workers. In the early years, patients might be exposed to radiation for long periods of time. Sometimes they held the film cassette while the x-ray was taken. People were also exposed to radiation daily while testing vacuum tubes, demonstrating equipment, positioning patients, and taking pictures. Radiographers often sat beneath tables holding x-ray equipment without protective shields. Moreover, in early machines, the direction of the beams could not be controlled well, increasing the risk of exposing numerous people, including medical personnel, patients, and visitors. Fluoroscopic examinations were especially hazardous, and during the 1890s, hand-held fluoroscopes were a common source of exposure to radiation.

The chemicals and equipment could be hazardous, too. Gas tubes sometimes exploded, causing cuts and flying bits of glass. People could shock themselves when they tripped on live electrical wires. Chemicals that gave off powerful odors were used to take x-rays and develop prints.

At first, people did not realize the risks of radiation. They also did not know that risks were higher for children and pregnant women. Doctors sometimes x-rayed babies to diagnose disease. X-rays were used for non-medical purposes, too, such as measuring children's feet in shoe stores.

As early as 1896, Elihu Thomson wrote about x-ray burns that did not heal. Radiographers and patients reported burns, eye problems, pain, numbness, and infection. A physician at Vanderbilt University lost his hair within weeks after his skull was radiographed. Another man developed skin burns and lost the hair on the side that was exposed to radiation during a skull x-ray. Writing for New York's *Medical Record,* one doctor noted cases of hair loss, lesions, and reddened or peeling flesh. He warned, "I wish to suggest that more be understood regarding the action of the x-rays before the general practitioner adopts them in his daily work."

Researchers were among the victims. American physicist Emile Grubbe severely burned his hands while experimenting with open Crookes tubes. Becquerel developed a burn on his chest after carrying a tube of radium salts in his breast pocket.

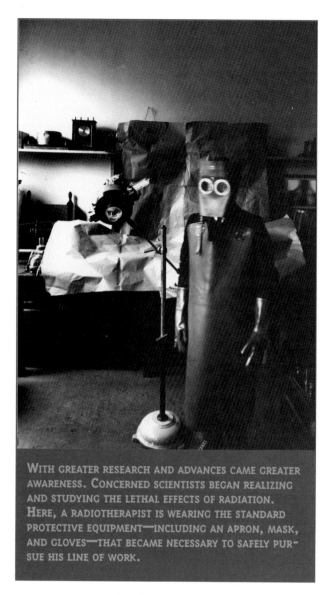

WITH GREATER RESEARCH AND ADVANCES CAME GREATER AWARENESS. CONCERNED SCIENTISTS BEGAN REALIZING AND STUDYING THE LETHAL EFFECTS OF RADIATION. HERE, A RADIOTHERAPIST IS WEARING THE STANDARD PROTECTIVE EQUIPMENT—INCLUDING AN APRON, MASK, AND GLOVES—THAT BECAME NECESSARY TO SAFELY PURSUE HIS LINE OF WORK.

Concerned scientists began studying the effects of radiation on animals. Their research showed that certain doses could be fatal. In 1902 a researcher reported that exposure had caused skin cancer. Other laboratory studies showed that radiation could kill the fetuses of experimental mammals and cause mutation in the genes of toads.

Some people downplayed the seriousness of these problems and suggested other causes, such as the electricity used in x-rays. Others took precautions by wearing protective devices and putting lead casing on their x-ray tubes. Dentists placed heavy glass plates over their eyes when working with x-rays. More companies offered protective gloves and aprons along with their x-ray machines. They made lead screens, aprons, and helmets, along with other items people could wear or place in their labs.

The first death blamed on radiation exposure was recorded in 1904. The victim was Clarence M. Dally, a researcher at Thomas Edison's lab in New Jersey. For several years, he had worked with x-rays, holding the tubes in his hands and placing his hands in front of the beams. He developed severe burns on both arms, followed by cancer. Doctors amputated Dally's arms to try and save his life. After he died, Edison announced that his lab would stop all radiation research. Edison also refused to have any x-rays taken of him for the rest of his life.

In 1905 Elizabeth Fleischmann perished at age forty-six. Still another well-known pioneer, Mihran Kassabian, died in 1910. Kassabian had developed the radiology lab at a Philadelphia hospital where he performed more than eight hundred x-rays during a two-year period. In 1900 he developed x-ray burns. Cancer was found in his left hand eight years later.

For several decades, people working in radiology continued to die from cancer at much higher rates than the general public. In addition to skin cancer, they displayed much higher rates of leukemia, a cancer of the blood. People debated whether or not x-rays caused cancer and, if they did, how. Some radiologists tried to learn more about the process by monitoring what happened to their bodies as they were dying. Mihran Kassabian photographed his hands and wrote about the changes as he developed burns, followed by necrosis (tissue death), leading to the amputations and then his death.

Radiologists called for safety standards, safer equipment, and more products to shield them from radiation. In 1915 the British Roentgen Society made the first organized effort to impose safety standards. Its x-ray and Radium Protection Committee published recommendations in 1921. The United States also developed safety standards. In 1924 Arthur Mutscheller suggested a limit on radiation exposure based on a "tolerance dose," which he defined as "the dose which an operator can, for a prolonged period of time, tolerate without ultimately suffering injury." Nobody knew what that exact dose was, however.

During the 1920s, radiologists worked to define certain terms that measured radiation: a roentgen (representing the amount of radiation emitted by an x-ray tube and directed into the target in order to obtain an image) and a curie (the amount of radiation emitted by a gram of radium). The International Commission on X-ray Units was formed for this purpose. The commission issued its report at a meeting in 1928, attended by representatives from numerous countries. Attendees decided on a standard roentgen—the amount of radioactivity that would produce one electrostatic unit of charge in 1 cubic centimeter (0.06 cubic inch) of air at 0 degrees Centigrade.

At that same meeting, the editor of the *American Journal of Roentgenology* presented the results of a questionnaire he had sent to American radiologists. Information gathered from 377 people revealed that 138 married radiologists were infertile (unable to have children). Among the children born to other respondents, physical abnormalities were twice as common as they were in the general population.

New organizations were formed to take action. The International Committee on X-ray and Radium Protection, established in 1928, was the forerunner of the International Committee on Radium Protection (ICRP). The next year, the U.S. Advisory Committee on X-ray and Radium Protection was formed; this later became the National Council on Radiation Protection and Measurement (NCRP). This committee published its first recommendations in 1931, stating that people should not be exposed to more than 0.2 R/day. The NCRP recommended that same limit in 1934 but later lowered its recommendation to 0.1 R/day and 0.5 R/week. By 1950 the limit had been lowered again to 0.3 R/week.

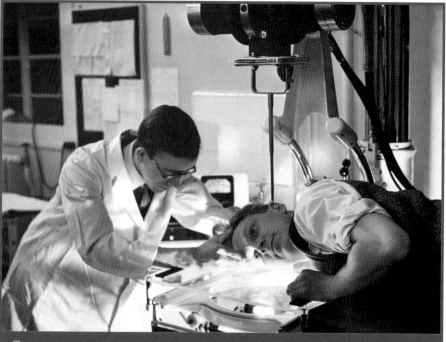

THE 1950S SAW INCREASED SCRUTINY GIVEN TO THE LONG-TERM EFFECTS OF EXPOSURE TO RADIATION. THIS TECHNICIAN AT ENGLAND'S HARWELL ATOMIC CENTER X-RAYS A WORKER WHO HAS BEEN EXPOSED TO RADIATION.

Research on the effects of radiation accelerated after World War II. During those years, thousands of people had worked with radioactive materials as they conducted research or produced materials for the atomic bomb project organized by the U.S. government. A study in 1956 showed a correlation between exposure to x-rays and childhood cancers. The evidence had accumulated for decades and was too strong to ignore.

Still other elements of the x-ray process proved harmful or dangerous as well. Flammable film posed a fire hazard in x-ray libraries and storage areas. During the 1920s, double emulsion film replaced glass photographic plates but nonflammable film did not provide as clear an image. A 1929 fire that began in the x-ray storage area at the Cleveland Clinic killed 124 people, raising even more concern about flammability. Within a few years, the Kodak and DuPont companies were selling safety film for X-rays.

Clearly, radiography had its major drawbacks. Scientists continued working to improve their safety and performance. The late twentieth century saw many changes in radiographic capabilities and stricter safety precautions, along with the arrival of exciting new imaging techniques.

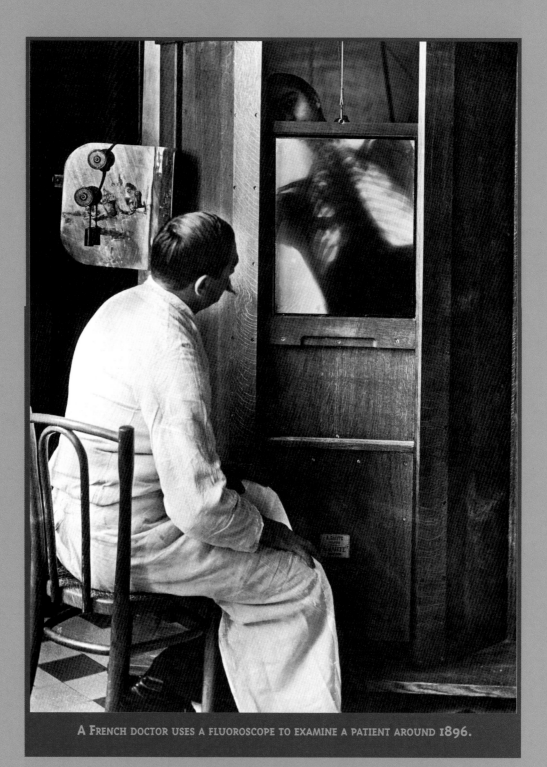

A FRENCH DOCTOR USES A FLUOROSCOPE TO EXAMINE A PATIENT AROUND 1896.

Live Images and New Views

From the earliest days of x-ray technology, people were aware of its limitations. The images were flat and shadowy and showed only dense body structures clearly. They did not differentiate among various soft tissues or show the organs hidden behind or beneath bones, such as the heart and brain. The blood vessels or spinal cord could not be viewed with x-rays alone. As scientists sought to improve x-ray technology, they looked for solutions to these problems. They found that adding certain substances to the body can provide enough contrast to highlight specific anatomical structures in x-ray images. This technique was used with standard x-rays and with the related technique of fluoroscopy.

The idea of a fluoroscope emerged shortly after Roentgen's announcement, and various people tried to make these devices. In March 1896, an Italian physicist described his apparatus, which had a tube with a fluorescent screen at one end and an eyepiece at the other. American inventor Thomas Edison developed a popular version of the hand-held fluoroscope. After testing more than eight thousand chemicals at his laboratory in West Orange, New Jersey, Edison found that calcium tungstate would fluoresce more strongly than the barium platinocyanide that was on the plate in Roentgen's lab. He also used thinner glass than the standard Crookes tube, and his electrodes were made from aluminum disks, not the usual platinum. X-rays traveled faster through Edison's fluoroscope. It produced accurate images and could be used along with an x-ray machine for making medical diagnoses.

Edison exhibited his fluoroscope in 1896 at the annual Electrical Exhibition in New York City. After entering a darkened room, visitors could look through a cushioned eyepiece into a curtained wooden box at a screen. There, they could see their own bones on the screen by placing a hand in front of the x-ray tube, as Roentgen's wife had once done.

With a fluoroscope, people could observe the image coming from the x-ray tube live, on a fluorescent screen. Doctors used fluoroscopes to examine a patient in real time, rather than waiting for film to be developed. The operator could pass the fluoroscope over an area of the body while watching the screen. The device could also be paired with a photographic plate to take pictures doctors could use for surgery and other treatment purposes.

While these developments were occuring, researchers also looked for ways of producing images of the brain, spinal cord, blood vessels, urinary tract, digestive tract, and other parts of the body. Contrast agents were used to highlight the particular areas and organs. Contrast agents are solutions of substances that look opaque when they are exposed to x-rays because they have a relatively high atomic weight. This approach was attempted as early as January 1896—but on dead bodies not live subjects. Mercury-based compounds were injected into blood vessels in order to illuminate them before taking x-ray photos. Other researchers tried, unsuccessfully, to view the esophagus by having people swallow small rubber bags containing lead.

Researchers continued to test materials that would be effective but also safe for use in organs and hollow or fluid-filled areas of the body, such as the bladder. In December 1896, a medical student (and future physiologist) Walter B. Cannon gave laboratory animals some bismuth salts orally. He then used a fluoroscope to view their intestines on the screen. The first contrast image of the kidneys was produced in 1906. Within a few years, doctors were able to see the blood vessels, bile ducts, gallbladder, and digestive and GI systems in a living person.

One widely used technique emerged in 1910, when researchers found a safe method of viewing the gastrointestinal (GI), or digestive, tract in humans. This tract starts at the throat and ends at the rectum. Patients were given a contrast agent called barium sulfate before x-rays were taken. For several decades, doctors ordered versions of this test (called the barium swallow, barium x-ray, or barium enema) for patients who experienced stomach pains, unexplained weight loss, blood coming from the rectum, or a change in bowel habits. These symptoms could signify cancer, polyps in the colon, ulcers, a narrowing of the esophagus, or a hiatal hernia, for example.

The procedure was usually done on an outpatient basis without anesthesia.

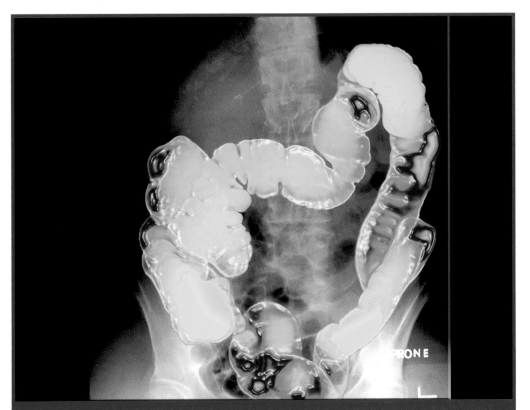

THIS COLOR-ENHANCED X-RAY SHOWS THE POWERFUL ENHANCEMENT ACHIEVED BY THE ADDITION OF BARIUM TO THE SYSTEM. A SMALL AMOUNT IS OFTEN USED TO COAT THE WALLS OF THE LARGE INTESTINE. AIR IS THEN INTRODUCED TO THE ORGAN, WHICH ALLOWS THE WALLS TO BE SHARPLY OUTLINED AND SEEN. SOME OF THE DISEASES AND CONDITIONS THAT CAN BE DIAGNOSED USING THIS METHOD INCLUDE COLON CANCER, INTESTINAL POLYPS, AND CHRON'S DISEASE, WHICH INVOLVES AN INFLAMMATION OF THE INTESTINAL TRACT.

Before a barium test, patients had to fast for a specific period of time or be given a purgative or enema so their intestines would be as empty as possible. They were given a drink containing barium sulfate, water, and flavoring, or the barium solution was introduced into the body through a tube. As the barium moved through the digestive tract, photos were taken at specific time intervals. Doctors could look at the illuminated organs through a fluoroscope or through still pictures and decide what was causing the problems.

New technology gave even better views of organs in action. Radiologist Alice Ettinger arrived in the United States from Germany in 1932 bringing the newly invented spot-film device. When used with the barium swallow, it showed successive fluoroscopic images of the GI tract. In addition, the machine could take still pictures as well as a successive series of images. Besides using this device to identify problems, doctors could monitor a patient's progress during treatment.

After 1960 endoscopy was also used as an alternative to the barium x-ray. During endoscopy, a narrow tube called an endoscope is inserted through a body orifice or an incision. At one time, the tubes were rigid but fiber-optic technology has resulted in the creation of more flexible ones. Narrower tubes can also now be made. With probes that measure about 1 millimeter (0.04 inch), some tubes are narrow enough to enter coronary arteries, the blood vessels found in the heart.

During an endoscopic exam of the upper gastrointestinal track, the tube is typically passed down the throat until it reaches the targeted area. A beam of light is sent down one of two tubes in the endoscope. The other tube carries the view to either an eyepiece attached to the other end or the image is revealed on a video screen. The endoscope also often has other instruments in one of its tubes allowing, for example, physicians to remove and retrieve a tissue sample. Optical equipment allows the doctor to view organs and body cavities. Rod lenses were first introduced in 1966. They offer better views than previous versions, which were based on the lenses used in telescopes.

Endoscopies can help physicians detect diseases, obstructions, and foreign objects. One example of the technology is endoscopic retrograde cholangiopancreatography (ERCP), which images ducts leading from the liver, gallbladder, and pancreas into the duodenum or the upper portion of the small intestine. This test is used to detect gallstones, cirrhosis of the liver, and cancer, or to detect duct irregularities caused by inflammation. It can also be done before gallbladder surgery to check for gallstones.

New endoscopes include microchip sensors that send data to a computer for analysis. Surgeons can use this information to perform laser surgery, which debuted in the 1960s. Lasers are used to remove tumors or cauterize ruptured blood vessels. They can also be used to remove a diseased gallbladder. The surgeon is able to watch a screen as the endoscope provides information to guide his or her work. Prior to this development, gallbladder surgery entailed a long incision across the abdomen and several days in the hospital, along with the risk of post-operative

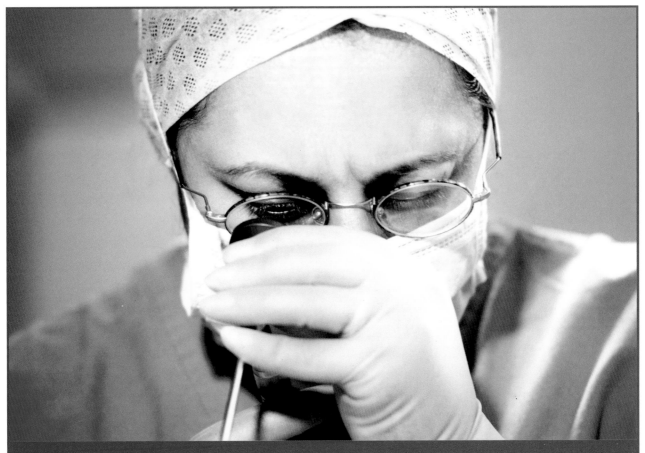

A SURGEON USES AN ENDOSCOPE, PEERING INTO AN OTHERWISE INACCESSIBLE ANATOMICAL AREA.

complications. New techniques allow for a shorter hospital stay and recovery period. A few small incisions are made in the abdomen, so there is no long or pronounced scar.

While some researchers were focusing on the GI tract, others sought ways of imaging the central nervous system—the brain and spinal cord. They found that air worked as an effective contrast medium in this area. In 1915 an x-ray was taken of the brain of a London woman who had told her doctor that she felt "splashing" inside her head. The x-ray showed fluid moving around in her cranium. Nine years earlier, surgeons had made a small hole in the woman's skull in order to remove a bony tumor near her eye. Apparently, air and water had moved that hole and accumulated through the years. Their presence provided some contrast that made it possible to see part of her brain with an x-ray.

In 1919 at Johns Hopkins University in Baltimore, Maryland, brain surgeon Walter Dandy tried injecting a harmless gas into cerebrospinal fluid so that he could radiograph the spine and brain. Using a special technique that became known as pneumoencephalography, he performed a lumbar puncture. With one needle, he removed some spinal fluid while a second needle injected air. The air he put into the spinal column rose to the ventricles of the brain. This technique enabled Dandy and other doctors to find lesions in the brain. They also could see abnormal fluid in the brains of infants. The accumulation of spinal fluid in the brain is called hydrocephalus. Dandy used a procedure called ventriculography to view the infants' brains. He utilized a spot on the skull where the bones do not fuse until several months after birth. By locating the fluid, doctors could remove it with a shunt, thus preventing brain damage and/or death.

Myelography—imaging the spinal column—saw its first significant advances during the 1920s. Jan Athanase Sicard of France found that lipiodol, a compound of iodine in oil, enabled him to image the spine using a fluoroscope. He could see tumors, bone spurs, and other problems associated with the spinal column. Sicard and his colleague Jacques Forestier then used this same contrast material to look at the bronchial tubes, uterus, bladder, and other organs. Iodine worked for this purpose because it has a high enough atomic density to block x-rays while the

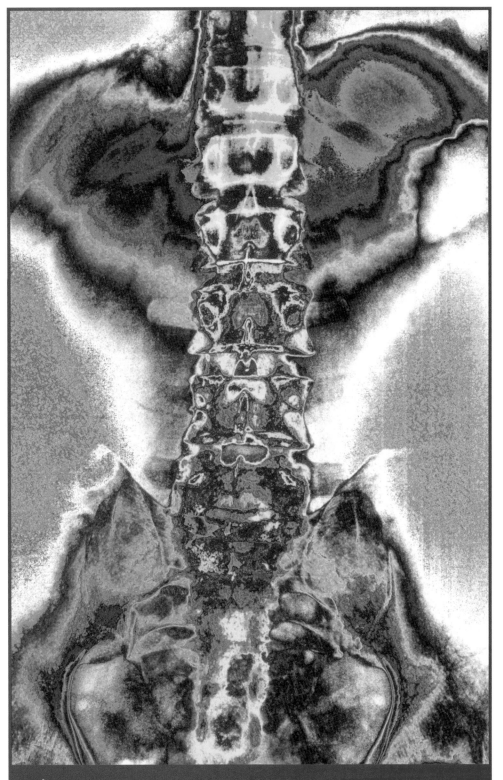

ADVANCES IN MYELOGRAPHY HAVE YIELDED DETAILED IMAGES OF THE INTRICACIES OF THE SPINAL CORD.

body can eliminate it naturally. Medical professionals continued using li-piodol into the 1940s. It proved unsuitable for imaging blood vessels, however, because it is oil based and could cause clotting.

In 1927 Portuguese neurologist Egas Moniz injected sodium iodide (salts of iodine) into the carotid arteries in order to view the blood vessels in the brain. He tried this technique with dogs and then humans. Moniz was able to see the cerebral arteries and tumors in the cerebrum. This marked the beginning of angiography—the imaging of blood vessels using a contrast medium. The first radiographic images of the gallbladder, bile duct, and their related blood vessels were also generated in the 1920s.

Some specialists began using thorium dioxide, yet another agent, for contrast x-rays because it gave a clearer image than iodine. The sub-stance was used into the 1950s. It led to serious health problems, how-ever, because the liver does not excrete thorium. Years after receiving this compound, people developed brain tumors and damage in the spleen and liver caused by long-term irradiation.

By the late 1920s doctors could perform cardiac catheterizations along with fluoroscopy. By 1945 physicians were able to generate images of the coronary arteries with contrast agents. This marked a milestone in angiography and provided essential information used for new surgical procedures and treatments. Angiography could provide "maps" of the heart that physicians used as a guide for performing open-heart surgery.

Another major innovation was the film cassette changer developed by George Schoenander. With this device, a series of cassettes could be exposed at a frame rate of 1.5 per second, similar to a motion picture. Other people worked to improve this technology. By 1953 a special cut film changer made the process even quicker, allowing rates of up to six frames per second.

Meanwhile, increasingly smaller parts of the body were being im-aged with contrast agents and fluoroscopy. The names of procedures specify the body part being imaged—for example, lymphoangiography (LAG) refers to examination of the lymph nodes. This procedure is done to check lymph nodes for cancer, since cancer cells from other or-gans can spread to nearby lymph nodes.

Radiography in general gained ground during the 1950s both in terms of safety and efficiency. Mirror optic systems were developed to reduce the amount of radiation present during procedures. The x-ray image intensifier arrived in 1955, just as television was reaching millions of American homes. A television camera connected to a monitor made it possible to produce an x-ray movie that showed bright, dynamic images on the screen. Doctors could watch the workings of the human heart and blood vessels more clearly than before.

Digital technology and new imaging tools made an impact during the 1970s. Radiology departments began using computers, and the field became increasingly specialized as new technology offered numerous imaging techniques that offered clear and detailed pictures of organ systems. One of the most exciting developments of the decade was the use of coronary angioplasty, which was first done in Switzerland. In the procedure, a catheter is threaded through an artery starting at the groin and ultimately reaching the heart. The doctor, watching on an x-ray screen, finds the blockage, inflates a balloon to compress the plaque and widen the artery, then withdraws the catheter. This procedure can reduce the constriction of these vessels that causes heart attacks.

Medical imaging also expanded its scope to encompass more tests in which early detection of a disease or condition holds the key to survival. One such procedure is mammography—the imaging of breast tissue. Millions of women around the world have had one or more mammograms. For years, organizations that study cancer have recommended that women older than age forty have a mammogram every one to two years. They also recommend that younger women who have a history of cancer or other high risk factors talk with their physician about having mammograms before age forty.

Mammography was developed in 1962 after research showed that radiography could find more breast tumors and smaller tumors than could manual exams. A study conducted starting in 1973 by the American Cancer Society and National Cancer Institute followed 280,000 women. Of the cancers detected in the women aged forty to forty-nine, about 90 percent were found by mammograms. Of the cancers detected

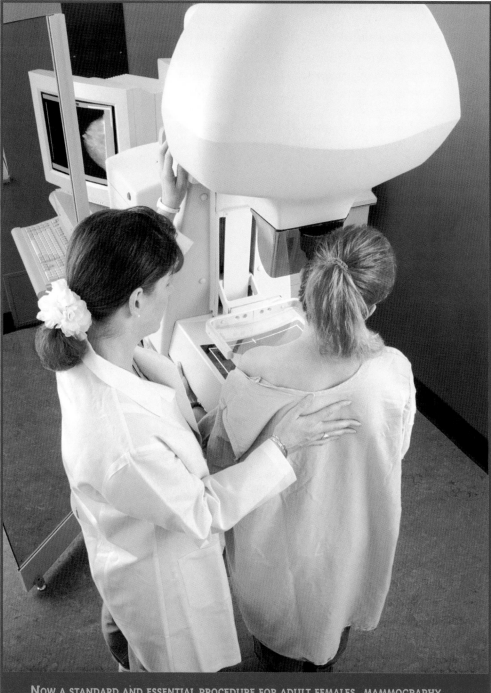

NOW A STANDARD AND ESSENTIAL PROCEDURE FOR ADULT FEMALES, MAMMOGRAPHY ALLOWS FOR THE EARLY DETECTION OF BREAST CANCER, WHICH CLAIMED AN ESTIMATE 40,000 AMERICAN WOMEN IN 2005.

in women aged fifty to fifty-nine, about 95 percent were found by mammograms. Critics point out that some radiation is involved in a mammogram. In response, advocates of mammography say that the dose is minimal. They contend that the risk of undetected breast cancer far exceeds any potential harm from the procedure itself. To ensure the safest possible procedure either way, the Food and Drug Administration (FDA) approved digital mammography in 2000.

By the late twentieth century, safety problems with x-rays had been minimized by better technology, greater awareness, and brief exposure times. Today's x-rays can be taken in just milliseconds and use only about 2 percent of the radiation they required a century ago. Machines are designed to prevent rays from harming health care staff or patients. People are still cautious, however. Pregnant women are told to avoid all x-rays and women of childbearing age who have dental or medical x-rays wear protective lead aprons as an extra precaution. People who work with x-rays wear protective gear and can leave the immediate area while the actual x-ray is taken, operating a switch outside the room.

Contrast agents are considered safe, although some patients experience an allergic reaction or other side effects. Iodine and barium are the most common contrast agents in use today. Newer contrast materials, including nonionic varieties, seem to cause fewer side effects.

X-rays continue to be a fast and efficient means of gathering certain kinds of information. The basic method of producing them still involves electrical power and an x-ray tube containing a source of electrons (a cathode) and an anode, now made from a thick tungsten disk. Negatively charged electrons are attracted to this anode and as they strike the disc, x-rays are emitted. These energetic rays emerge as a beam from a small opening in the lead casing around the x-ray tube.

Of course, traditional radiography is now just one of many imaging techniques. Newer methods, including ultrasound, CT, MRI, nuclear medicine, and PET, offer tools for medical diagnosis and treatment that people might never have imagined a century ago. Just as Roentgen's mysterious rays revolutionized medical practice at the turn of the twentieth century, these developments have had a huge impact on modern health care.

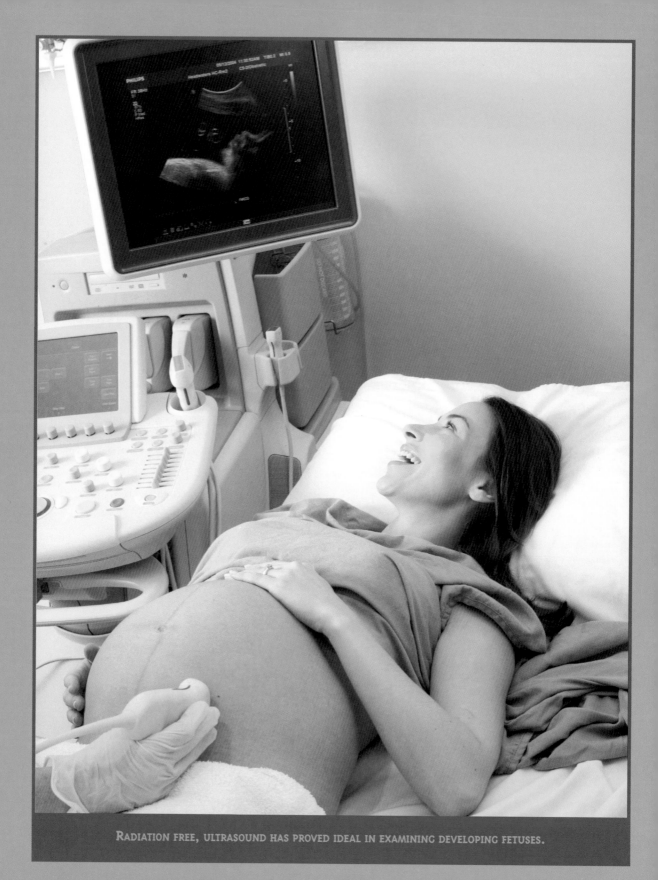

RADIATION FREE, ULTRASOUND HAS PROVED IDEAL IN EXAMINING DEVELOPING FETUSES.

Medical Ultrasound

Since the invention of photography, parents have cherished the first images takes on their newborns, often captured immediately after birth. Today, many people born after 1970 also have a photograph of themselves taken *before* they were born. During the pregnancy, their mother was given an ultrasound scan that produced a "baby picture" called a sonogram. This procedure can yield important, sometimes life-saving information about the growth and development of a fetus inside the womb.

Ultrasound is one of the imaging techniques that do not rely on radiation. Instead, ultrasound and a related technique called Doppler ultrasound produce images based on the detection of echoes returned from sound waves that are passed through the body. This technology is used to image many other organs and areas of the body beside the uterus. After x-rays, ultrasound is the most common type of medical imaging. Millions of ultrasounds are performed each year in the United States alone.

Known as ultrasound imaging, ultrasound scanning, or sonography, this procedure is relatively inexpensive and quick. Patients experience minimal discomfort. The equipment is portable, so it can be taken to people who are unable to travel to a medical facility.

Like the radar used in aviation and the sonar (an acronym for *so*und *na*vigation *r*anging) that helps submarines navigate in deep waters, ultrasound technology is based on the scientific principles governing sound waves. Sound waves travel through air, water, and other matter at different speeds, depending on the medium through which they are moving. Animals have made use of the principles of ultrasound for thousands of years. Bats use echolocation (biological sonar) to navigate in the dark and locate insects and other prey. They emit high frequency sound waves from their mouths and noses. This helps them to identify the types and locations of various objects by the kind of sound echo that comes back. Whales and dolphins also use echolocation to determine the nature of objects in their underwater environment.

During World War I, the Allied forces had a similar need to locate the presence of often difficult-to-detect enemy submarines. Scientists assigned the task made rapid progress in developing the ultrasonic underwater detection system known as sonar (an acronym for sound navigation and ranging). French physicist Pierre Langevin made an ultrasound generator and found that this technique worked well in water, since sound waves move through that medium in a fairly predictable way.

Other scientists experimented with ultrasound, too. At the University of Michigan, Floyd Firestone developed what he called a "reflectoscope." This device had the capacity to send out and detect sound waves all in a single instrument. In 1937 Austrian neurologist Karl Dussik and his physicist brother Friedrich managed to transmit attenuated sound waves through a man's head. They placed the ultrasound source on one side and the detector on the other. The Dussiks had hoped to produce an image of the brain, but the bones of the skull prevented the sound waves from passing through.

Sonar technology played a major role in the military arena during World War II (1939–1945). After the conflict ended, people found other uses for sonar. They bought discarded military equipment and used it for commercial purposes, including the detection of flaws in metals. As more people learned about sonar, curious innovators decided to find out if it might prove helpful in medical imaging. As scientists embarked on this new research, they wondered whether ultrasound could harm people, since exposure to continuous high-intensity ultrasound can damage living tissue. Despite the concerns, important breakthroughs were accomplished. During the 1940s, English surgeon John Wild came up with a method of sending short pulses of sound waves. Known as the "pulse-echo" technique, this innovation made it possible for the transducer that sent out sound waves to also receive the echoes that came back. Wild's research revealed that different tissues reflect different signals. Later, Wild would find a way to incorporate water into the transducer so that patients no longer had to sit immersed in a tub.

Other people made important contributions to this growing field. A group of researchers at the Massachusetts Institute of Technology (MIT) developed an ultrasonic probe that was capable of locating gallstones. Still other researchers found ways to focus high-frequency sound waves and create images from the data gathered by ultrasound. Meanwhile, Swedish physician Lars Leksell was using ultrasound to diagnose problems in the brain. He detected a hematoma—a swollen area that results when a blood vessel breaks—in the brain of a one-year-old child by using ultrasound instruments that were designed to find flaws in metals. Leksell had reasoned that the bones of a baby's skull are thinner than those of adults so the waves would be able to penetrate. He also found an area of the adult skull that is thinner than the rest. By using ultrasound in a specific manner on that spot, he could identify a particular echo that indicated the presence of a tumor or other abnormal structure in the brain.

Dr. Ian Donald, an obstetrician-gynecologist in Scotland, hoped to use ultrasound with his pregnant patients. He had noted the similarity between a submarine in the water and a fetus floating in embryonic fluid in the womb. Donald worked on a device that he could use to image the growing fetus *in utero*—inside the womb. During his early experiments with ultrasound devices, Donald found a way to produce images of abdominal tumors. In 1955 he demonstrated that ultrasound could differentiate between ovarian cysts and fibroid tumors based on their differing echo patterns. The next year, Donald tried using ultrasound to diagnose disorders in a growing fetus.

The first ultrasound machines for diagnostic purposes debuted in the 1950s. For these early ultrasound tests, patients sat in tubs filled with water. Practical problems with the equipment and procedures kept ultrasound from being widely used in medical practice until the 1970s. The first images were lines and spikes on a graph, not pictures. Ultrasound pictures from the early 1960s show rough black-and-white images. Over the next decade, the pictures appeared in shades of gray and became clearer, though still somewhat fuzzy and meaningless to an untrained eye.

Further research and development brought ultrasound devices that worked faster and more efficiently. Although medical ultrasound was slow to reach the public, by the 1970s it was changing obstetrical medicine. Doctors were pleased to have a new tool for examining the soft tissues and organs that do not vary enough in their density to show up on an x-ray. They anticipated using ultrasound to examine the heart and abdomen, as well as for obstetrics and gynecology. Furthermore, ultrasound equipment was reasonably priced—about the same amount of money as an x-ray machine—and there was no ionizing radiation involved.

By the 1960s, the hazards of radiation had been widely publicized. People were especially concerned about the use of x-rays during pregnancy. A report released in 1956 had shown a strong connection between radiation exposure during pregnancy and childhood cancer. Despite concerns about the dangers of radiation, doctors had been x-raying pregnant women since 1896, a practice that continued into the 1950s. In most cases, these doctors wanted to know if a woman was carrying more than one fetus. In other cases, they hoped to resolve problems that occurred during pregnancy. Some doctors also used x-rays routinely to estimate due dates. But the rising fears about radiation exposure provided yet another reason to use ultrasound imaging.

To conduct an ultrasound, the practitioner first applies a special gel to the skin or in the general area that is being scanned. The gel helps

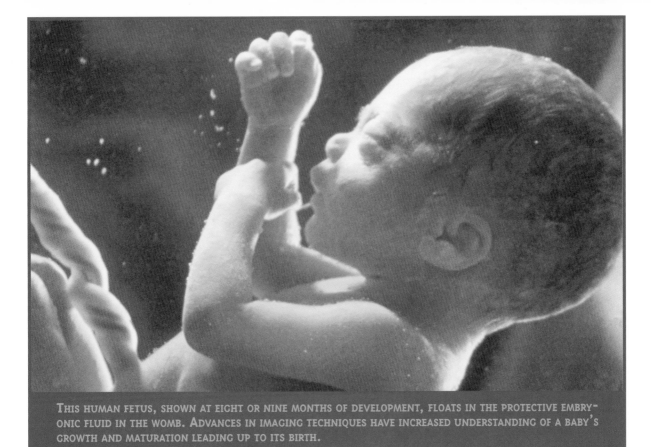

the instrument make better contact with the skin. An instrument called a transducer is placed against the skin to direct the ultrasound toward the organ or cavity being examined. This small instrument is moved around the target area in a series of arc-shaped lines. The transducer acts like a microphone to detect and receive sound. It sends out high-frequency sound waves that cannot be heard by the human ear. As they penetrate the body, the ultrasound machine gathers information from returning sound waves as they bounce back or echo from various organs and body structures.

An image can be made from the various responses as the different types of tissue reflect waves in their own particular way. The nature of the echoes and their timing provide the key information. The ultrasound machine processes the returning sound waves into electrical signals. These signals are analyzed to create an image of the structures being examined. With the aid of computers and specially designed software, the machine turns this information it gathers into pictures. Today, ultrasound machines use computers and reconstruction software to create live pictures. These images are clearer than those made decades ago and can be produced in color as well.

Ultrasound has proved its usefulness in examining many areas of the body. It is especially helpful when radiation must be avoided, such as in examining pregnant women, babies, and children. It is often the preferred choice over certain other diagnostic procedures. If a medical condition can be effectively analyzed either through the use of x-rays, a CT scan, an MRI, or other type of imaging, ultrasound will likely be chosen because it costs less, is more convenient, and does not involve ionizing radiation.

Ultrasound also became an important tool in obstetric medicine. At the end of the twentieth century, about half of all ultrasounds were being done during pregnancy. Today's ultrasounds can show detailed images of the uterus and growing fetus, even the fine details of eyelashes and fingertips. The ultrasound will show, first of all, whether there is a multiple pregnancy (more than one fetus). It can also be used to confirm that a fetus has died in cases where there is no heartbeat or other sign of life.

During a routine fetal ultrasound, the head, spine, heart, kidneys, stomach, and bladder are examined, as well as the umbilical cord and placenta. This provides information about the progress and condition of the pregnancy, including the fetus's breathing, urination, and movements. Determining the size of the skull and the abdomen helps doctors to estimate the fetus's age. If the fetus is old enough and is positioned in a certain way, the gender can also be determined.

Many obstetricians administer more than one ultrasound to a patient during her pregnancy. Those done in the later weeks show whether the fetus is in the proper position for a normal vaginal delivery, with the head in the lower portion of the uterus so that it can emerge first. Doctors also have been able to perform an endovaginal or transvaginal exam in the early stages of certain women's pregnancies. For this test, the transducer is placed into the vagina for views of the fetus that cannot be obtained through an abdominal ultrasound.

Women may choose to have an ultrasound to help find out if their fetus has certain congenital abnormalities. During an amniocentesis, fluid is removed from the amniotic sac that encloses and protects the fetus inside the uterus. In a procedure called chorionic villus sampling, which can be performed early in the pregnancy, cells are extracted from the placenta. Tests are then done to examine the cells' chromosomes7. A number of genetic and developmental abnormalities can be identified this way, and the gender of the fetus can be determined as well. The picture that the ultrasound produces guides the person who is drawing the sample fluid so that the needle does not touch the fetus.

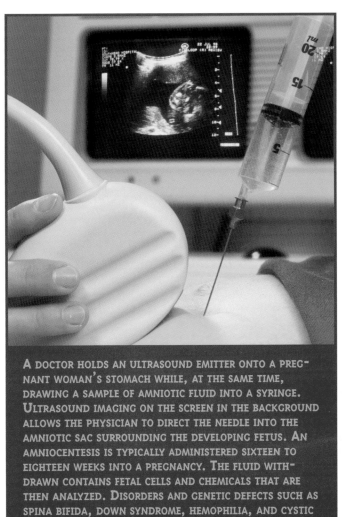

A DOCTOR HOLDS AN ULTRASOUND EMITTER ONTO A PREGNANT WOMAN'S STOMACH WHILE, AT THE SAME TIME, DRAWING A SAMPLE OF AMNIOTIC FLUID INTO A SYRINGE. ULTRASOUND IMAGING ON THE SCREEN IN THE BACKGROUND ALLOWS THE PHYSICIAN TO DIRECT THE NEEDLE INTO THE AMNIOTIC SAC SURROUNDING THE DEVELOPING FETUS. AN AMNIOCENTESIS IS TYPICALLY ADMINISTERED SIXTEEN TO EIGHTEEN WEEKS INTO A PREGNANCY. THE FLUID WITHDRAWN CONTAINS FETAL CELLS AND CHEMICALS THAT ARE THEN ANALYZED. DISORDERS AND GENETIC DEFECTS SUCH AS SPINA BIFIDA, DOWN SYNDROME, HEMOPHILIA, AND CYSTIC FIBROSIS CAN BE DETECTED IN THIS WAY.

The use of ultrasound in obstetrical medicine sparked the new field of prenatal surgery and the treatment of certain other medical problems while a fetus is still in the womb. For example, doctors can use a needle with suction to drain excess fluid from the fetus's brain. They can also deliver certain medications that work inside the womb. Doctors also use the information from ultrasound to plan neonatal surgery. They can identify heart problems and defects in the neural tube (the developing central nervous system) less than halfway through the pregnancy. Or, an ultrasound might reveal a tumor that threatens the safety and health of the fetus. In cases like these, the baby can be delivered as soon as it is mature enough to survive and can then undergo immediate surgery. If treatment can wait until the pregnancy comes to term, doctors will know ahead of time that they must schedule neonatal surgery and what they need to do.

When a woman complains of pelvic pain, an ultrasound may be done to look for tumors, cysts, abscesses, internal bleeding, pelvic inflammatory disease, or ectopic pregnancy. Ectopic pregnancy, in which the fertilized egg grows outside the uterus, can be serious. In 20 percent of these cases, the patient is not diagnosed until an emergency situation occurs. This can result in internal bleeding of the arteries leading to the uterus. The fallopian tube, which carries eggs from the ovary to the uterus, may rupture. These kinds of complications may leave a woman unable to bear children. They can even result in death.

Ultrasounds can also help pinpoint the causes of infertility—the inability to bear children. Certain kinds of tumors or cysts may prevent a woman from being able to get pregnant or to sustain a pregnancy after fertilization occurs. Surgery and other treatments can alleviate many of these problems.

In addition to gynecology and obstetrics, ultrasound also works well for imaging the heart and blood vessels, pelvis, male reproductive organs, kidneys, liver, pancreas, gallbladder, eye, and thyroid gland. It offers a noninvasive way to find gallstones. The gallbladder is a small sac located in the right upper abdomen. It stores bile, a substance that is made in the liver and is released into the intestines through a narrow duct when the bile is needed to aid in the digestion of fats. Sometimes bile hardens into small stonelike formations that cause intense pain as they pass from the gallbladder into the intestine. An ultrasound can produce images that show the number and size of stones inside the gallbladder. It can also show the condition of the gallbladder itself, including signs of inflammation or the presence of deposits on the walls. Likewise, an ultrasound may show damage in the kidneys or reveal abnormalities of the colon.

Ultrasounds are used in sports medicine or other situations when people have soft-tissue or superficial injuries. The procedure can also show the trapped or swollen nerves in the wrist that result from carpal tunnel syndrome, as well as certain kinds of nerve damage, injured ligaments, or a torn rotator cuff in the shoulder.

An ultrasound may pinpoint the cause of eye problems. It can help doctors diagnose, for example, a detached retina, which occurs when the retina is pulled away from its normal position inside the back wall of the eyeball. The retina is the part of the eye that translates light signals into nerve signals, so a detached retina can lead to blindness. An ultrasound that shows the area behind the eye may also reveal tumors, hemorrhages, or other problems.

Doctors use ultrasounds to diagnose cancer in the lymph nodes, breast, liver, pelvis, brain, and other places. Another important use is checking the prostate gland, a male reproductive organ, for cancer. Since this particular kind of cancer is so common in the United States in men older than age sixty, some clinics offer free ultrasound screenings during Prostate Cancer Awareness Month each September. For breast examinations, ultrasound may be performed to provide additional information, typically after potential problems have been revealed in a mammogram. This may be especially useful when women have dense breast tissue or breast implants. In addition to showing a tumor or mass, the information gathered from an ultrasound can guide the professionals who take samples of tissues during a biopsy. These tissue cells are then tested to determine whether cells from a tumor are malignant (cancerous) or not.

In the operating room, ultrasounds can guide the surgeon at work. They also are used after surgery to investigate complications. For example, if a patient experiences unusual pain after surgery, an ultrasound may show the cause, such as fluid buildup or scar tissue forming around the site.

In recent years, more ultrasounds are being done to diagnose and treat heart disease, heart attacks, or vascular disease (affecting the blood vessels) that might lead to a stroke. Heart disease is the leading cause of death in the United States, and many ultrasounds are performed to look for damage in the heart or blood vessels as well as congenital abnormalities.

The area of ultrasound called Doppler ultrasound is especially useful for studying the flow of blood in veins and arteries. This technology is named for Austrian physicist Christian Johann Doppler who described

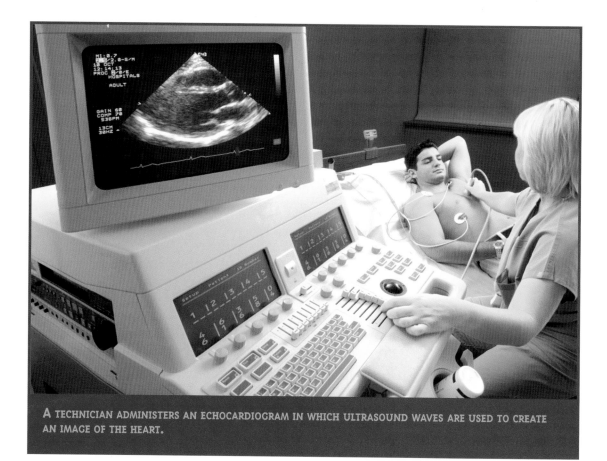

what is called the Doppler effect in 1842. It refers to the changing frequency of sound as an object moves from a given point. Doppler techniques have been used in astronomy to study the distances among objects in the solar system, as well as in weather forecasting and in law enforcement, where it is used to calculate an automobile's speed.

During the 1950s, Japanese researchers Shigeo Satomura and Yasuharu Nimura at Osaka University tried sending ultrasound into a blood vessel. They theorized that the speed of blood would be faster in an unclogged blood vessel. This meant that measuring the speed could provide valuable information about the condition of the arteries and the valves of the heart. Around the world, other scientists worked on similar projects. The development of this technology had to wait, however. Processing all the information from such tests required the power of a computer.

Once computers became more functional and widely used, Doppler ultrasound enjoyed an enthusiastic reception. The information collected by Doppler ultrasound can show how well blood is moving through a vessel, and whether the flow is smooth or irregular, just as sounds would change when water moves through a clear pipe or one that is clogged. Different sounds occur, depending on the degrees of obstruction. Doppler ultrasound helps to diagnose occlusion—blockage—in an artery or an embolism. About 80 percent of all heart attacks result from coronary artery disease, making this one of the most serious of all health problems. Doppler ultrasound can image the carotid artery to check for the presence of the plaque that signals this disease.

Cardiologists have relied on the Doppler echocardiogram to detect certain kinds of heart disease, including those resulting from valve defects or coronary artery disease. An echocardiogram can show the presence of heart murmurs and a condition known as mitral valve prolapse—an anatomical irregularity in which the heart's mitral valve does not close normally. Various medical and holistic treatments can be prescribed to address and target the symptoms.

New developments such as Duplex and color Doppler ultrasound make it possible to determine the depth of the vessel that is sending back a particular echo signal. As more and more heart-focused ultrasounds are performed, scans of the cardiovascular system may become even more common than prenatal ultrasounds.

Doppler ultrasound has also proved helpful with cancer detection as doctors are able to spot the changes that occur in blood vessels during the early stages of a malignancy. In an interview with author Howard Sochurek, Dr. Christopher Merritt of the Ochsler Clinic in New Orleans commented, "Cancer induces the formation of new blood vessels which are not normal. We will look at the tissues that are supplied by these blood vessels which may be some of the earliest changes we can perceive." Without the development of these various techniques and procedures, doctors would often not be able to provide their patients with the precise care they need.

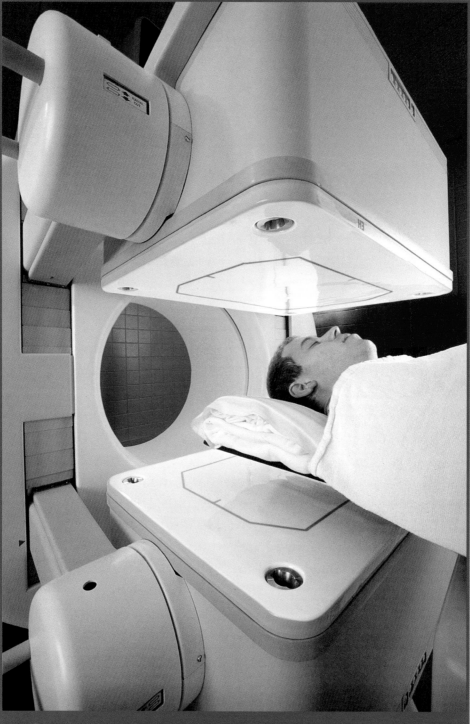

COMPUTERIZED AXIAL TOMOGRAPHY, BETTER KNOWN AS A **CAT** SCAN. CROSS-SECTIONAL AND THREE-DIMENSIONAL VIEWS OF TARGETED AREAS OF THE BODY ARE GENERATED.

CT Scans

The world-renowned geneticist and Nobel laureate James D. Watson once called the brain "the last and greatest biological frontier." During the 1970s, people were excited to see the soft tissue structures of the living brain for the first time. CT scanning, also called CAT, which stands for computerized axial tomography, made that possible. CT can be used for imaging just about any body structure or organ, including bones, soft tissue, organs, blood vessels, the spinal column, and the brain. It performs many functions that take imaging far beyond traditional x-rays and, as a result, has become a mainstay in medical-imaging departments.

Tomography comes from the Greek word *tomos* meaning "slice" or "section" and the word *graphia,* which means "to write or draw." For centuries, people understood the mathematical principles behind tomographic reconstruction, but this process required the power of computers, so CT was not possible before the digital revolution.

Basically, a CT scan is a special type of imaging test with scanners that move around the body. It provides cross-sectional and three-dimensional views of various areas using x-rays and the complex technology of the digital computer. A human operator gives the computer basic instructions regarding the number of slices to take and their thickness, the angles, and other aspects of the scan. The computer can then translate the signals into pixels that appear on a screen forming an instant image for real-time viewing. The computer can also enhance the CT scan images in various ways.

The idea of using tomography for medical imaging dates back to the early 1900s when people experimented with moving x-rays that took pictures at an angle. These researchers were attempting to see isolated interior portions of the body in order to produce images of tissues that were not visible because other tissues stood in the way. During the 1930s, one scientist experimented with this technique by moving the x-ray tube and film while keeping the targeted area in the same place. He was unable to capture the images he wanted, however. Decades later, in the 1960s, a series of rotating and translating detectors were developed for use in nuclear-medicine imaging.

CT technology able to provide medical imaging arrived in the 1970s, a time when medicine saw significant advances, such as the arrival of magnetic resonance imaging (MRI). Developments in other scientific fields suggested the possibility of computer-reconstructed pictures. This technology was being used to take pictures of the Moon during missions to outer space, for example.

CT machines, first known as CAT, were developed in 1972 by Godfrey Hounsfield at EMI Laboratories in England and by a South African–born physicist, Allan Cormack, of Tufts University. Working independently, these two scientists later jointly received the Nobel Prize for physiology or medicine in 1979 for their achievements.

CAT devices could detect acute differences in x-ray transparency among different soft tissues and then, with the aid of a computer, emphasize these differences to produce an image. The basic algorithms used in reconstructing CAT images came from Johann Radon, an Austrian mathematician. Radon developed these theories during the early 1900s and published a paper on the subject in 1917.

When the first CT scanners were made in labs in 1974, they were used to produce images of the head. For a while, the machines were as clumsy as they were slow. The ray detector was mounted on a rotating frame along with a digital computer so that cross-sectional images could be made of the targeted areas. The early machines required several hours to gather the data for just one "slice," and it took days to reconstruct the image.

Dr. Robert Ledley developed the first "all-body" CAT scanning technology, which became available to patients in 1976. Ledley designed a machine that showed images in different colors, saying that this enabled him to clarify and differentiate what he was observing. The companies that produced the technology used black and white, however. Ledley later said that perhaps the manufacturers thought that color pictures looked less scientific. At any rate, in these early CT images, dense tissues appeared white, while less dense tissues (for example, those making up the brain and muscles) appeared in shades of gray. Spaces filled with air looked black.

The use of CT grew rapidly. By the late 1970s, about six thousand scanners were in operation in the United States and the numbers kept growing. Users noted that CT surpassed X-rays by revealing more details. It showed hundreds of levels of contrast among various tissues—bone, soft tissue, organs—while x-rays detect only several different levels. The scanner could be tilted to show an array of views, varying angles of tissues, and three dimensions of the subject. The imaging process also involves exposure to more radiation. CT could be used to confirm an initial diagnosis made from x-rays.

Much of the initial excitement occurred because CT offered the chance to produce images of the brain, a process that differs from many other kinds of imaging because the brain does not have moving parts like the heart, lungs, or intestines. CT was a valuable tool for diagnosing tumors, bleeding, aneurysms, and injuries. It also proved indispensable in detecting tumors of the neck as well as enlarged lymph nodes or glands in the neck and chest. CT imaging helped doctors diagnose and treat cancer since it showed the relationship of the tumor to the surrounding organs. Scans of the sinuses could reveal obstructions or a narrowing of the openings that drain the sinuses, as well as other problems in the area. Before CT, it was nearly impossible to create an image of the pancreas—an abdominal organ that secretes important digestive enzymes. As a result, pancreatic cancers were not discovered until the disease had progressed into the later stages.

Although the first commercial MR (magnetic resonance) scanner was used in 1980, CT was still the main screening tool for cortical bone and fractures, body and chest imaging, and abdominal and pelvic disorders. CT can also be used to view the spine when patients complain of pain in the neck, back, arms, or legs. In spinal imaging, CT scans are able to show bulging or herniated disks or spinal stenosis (a narrowing of the spinal canal). After an accident, a scan may be done to check for fractures or breaks in the spinal column or other areas. CT scans also can show damage to the internal organs, such as the liver, kidneys, or spleen.

As with x-rays, contrast agents can be used with CT to examine the blood vessels. For this technique, called dynamic CT scanning, the contrast agent is injected into a vein before the test. Because CT technology can construct "slices" of body tissues and distinguish among bone, fat, and muscle, it can help doctors find blood clots and tumors.

Scans may take about two to five seconds each, or even less time with more advanced CT machines. During a CT scan, the patient lies on a sliding table that moves into the opening of the machine. For certain conditions, a contrast medium containing iodine may be administered so blood vessels or specific organs are more pronounced during the imaging process. Before an abdominal scan, patients may not be permitted to eat or drink anything for four to six hours, then given a barium solution so the intestinal tract shows up better.

The imaging device sends multiple x-ray pulses through a specific location on the body in order to transmit information to the computer. The source of the x-rays inside the scanner sends out a series of narrow (low-dosage) x-ray beams at different angles while the CT tube rotates around the patient. Detectors on the sides of the scanner pick up the radiation that is emitted as the thin, fan-shaped beams pass through various tissues.

The detectors then send the signals to a computer, which must be capable of processing millions of bytes of information per second as it directs the scanning process and receives and records information. Once the computer processes this data, the information can be saved, transmitted to other health care systems, or printed out as one or more photographs.

New technology has steadily improved the speed of CT scanning and

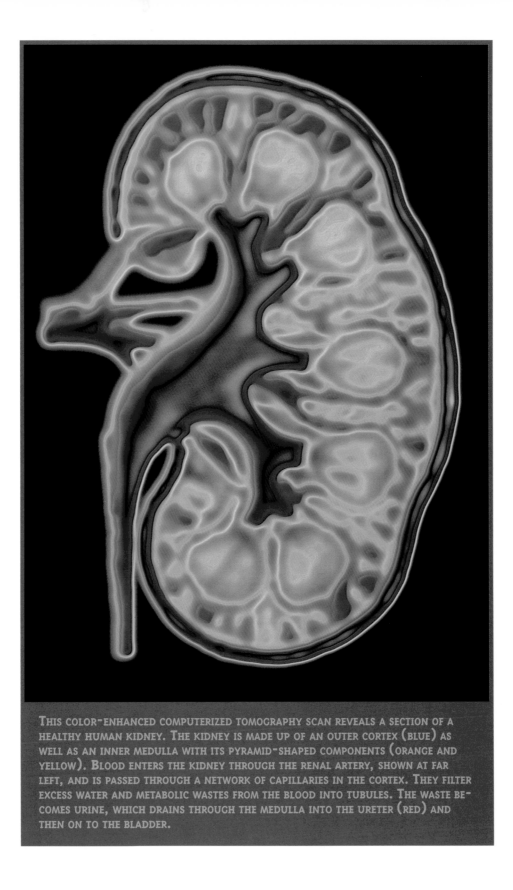

THIS COLOR-ENHANCED COMPUTERIZED TOMOGRAPHY SCAN REVEALS A SECTION OF A HEALTHY HUMAN KIDNEY. THE KIDNEY IS MADE UP OF AN OUTER CORTEX (BLUE) AS WELL AS AN INNER MEDULLA WITH ITS PYRAMID-SHAPED COMPONENTS (ORANGE AND YELLOW). BLOOD ENTERS THE KIDNEY THROUGH THE RENAL ARTERY, SHOWN AT FAR LEFT, AND IS PASSED THROUGH A NETWORK OF CAPILLARIES IN THE CORTEX. THEY FILTER EXCESS WATER AND METABOLIC WASTES FROM THE BLOOD INTO TUBULES. THE WASTE BE-COMES URINE, WHICH DRAINS THROUGH THE MEDULLA INTO THE URETER (RED) AND THEN ON TO THE BLADDER.

the quality of the images. One major advance in 1989 was the advent of spiral scanning. It allows rapid scanning of an area of the body in less than a minute. By 1998 quad-slice scanners were available, able to acquire four slices for each tube rotation. These units were followed by CT scanners that could take eight slices at a time.

Sophisticated CT technology has given surgeons more effective tools for planning procedures, such as hip replacements or reconstructive surgery in which broken bones, fractured skulls, or congenital hip defects are repaired or corrected. Using CT images, surgeons can make three-dimensional models before they operate, using CT images to construct replacement parts. For hip-replacement surgery, scans of the patient's hip and pelvis help determine the size and shape of the new parts. CT also proves valuable in carrying out difficult procedures where small errors can be disastrous for patients. One example is eye surgery that involves a tumor on the optic nerve. A precise three-dimensional model showing the precise structure of the eye and the tumor can guide the surgeon in performing this delicate operation. CT scans also inform caregivers about the effects of surgery and other treatments.

Recent years have brought even greater volumetric CT-scanning capabilities. Machines able to collect up to sixteen slices per scan were introduced in 2002. These devices outperform spiral scanners and allow for the fast and consistent imaging of the heart and blood vessels, as well as other imaging tasks.

Multislice CT systems (MSCT) can

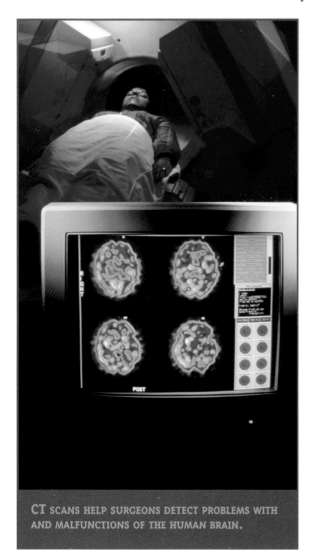

CT SCANS HELP SURGEONS DETECT PROBLEMS WITH AND MALFUNCTIONS OF THE HUMAN BRAIN.

collect data and assemble matrix images from millions of data points in less than one second. It now takes fewer than five seconds to scan an entire chest (totaling about forty slices) and fewer than ten seconds to scan a person's lower spine, as opposed the approximately forty-five minutes it took ten years ago. Accelerated scanning speed offers greater convenience for patients and physicians. It also means that images are finished before additional movements occur in the body due to functions such as breathing and swallowing. Within seconds, scanners can acquire and reconstruct images of a certain area.

The MDCT—multidetector CT—has fostered significant clinical advances, including enhanced studies of the vascular system. With MDCT, doctors can do a virtual endoscopy of the aorta (the heart's main artery), surgical reconstruction, and more accurate evaluation of pulmonary embolisms. Dr. Elliot K. Fishman, director of diagnostic radiology and body CT at Johns Hopkins Medical Center, said "CT angiography is the biggest clinical advance made possible by MDCT technology. In our practice, we are doing 15 to 20 of them per day now."

Furthermore, developments in software have allowed images of higher resolution to be produced. This, in turn, enables more accurate diagnoses and treatment plans. The computer can color the features of the image based on tissue density. It can enlarge and magnify, zoom in, show more contrast, and vary the colors, among other features.

During the early twenty-first century, CT technology offered an ever-increasing array of clinical uses and options for archiving, accessing, and displaying medical images. As of 2005, there were CT scanners in about 30,000 hospitals, outpatient facilities, and imaging centers around the world and the number was rapidly rising.

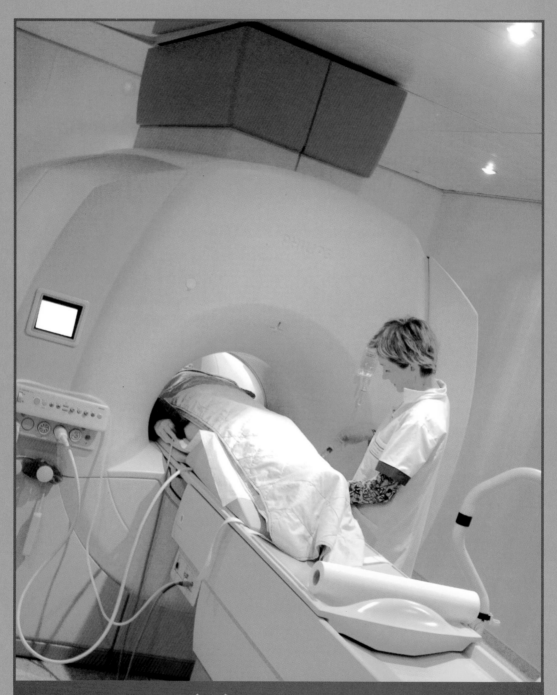

MAGNETIC RESONANCE IMAGING (MRI) IS YET ANOTHER PROCEDURE THAT HAS REVOLUTIONIZED THE CAPABILITIES OF THE MEDICAL WORLD. HERE, A TECHNICIAN MONITORS A PATIENT UNDERGOING AN MRI OF THE BACKBONE.

Magnetic Resonance Imaging

Some patients may feel intimidated when they arrive for an MRI—magnetic resonance imaging—scan. The scanner looks formidable, and people may feel claustrophobic as they find their entire bodies being placed inside the opaque "tunnel." Yet the procedure itself is painless, and most MR scans take just a few minutes. A patient may feel a slight tingling sensation during the scan itself and hear tapping or clicking noises that come from preparing the magnetic coils.

MRIs are used for numerous purposes, especially for evaluating tissues that have been biochemically altered. Experts have called MRI one of the most useful and promising types of medical imaging.

MRI uses a powerful magnetic field and radio waves to produce visual representations. Radiography, fluoroscopy, and CT create images by detecting variations in electron density, since this value varies from one tissue to another. MRI does something else. It is a special form of NMR—nuclear magnetic resonance.

The technology evolved from knowledge about magnetism that has been accumulating since ancient times. A major breakthrough occurred during the 1860s, when Scottish scientist James Clerk Maxwell developed a unified theory of electromagnetism. He showed that waves of electromagnetic energy can penetrate both matter and empty space. His experiments showing the close relationship between electric and magnetic fields laid the groundwork for the later development of wireless communication, as well as x-rays.

The scientific principles underlying this imaging technique were known by the 1940s. Physicists Felix Bloch and Edward Purcell discovered nuclear magnetic resonance in 1945 and later won the Nobel Prize in Physics in 1952 for their work. These scientists explored the effects of radio pulses on protons in a strong magnetic field. The electromagnetic radiation that is present can be detected. When magnetic resonance is used in the human body, beams of radio energy are directed at hydrogen atoms so that their nuclei will resonate. Hydrogen is a good choice for this purpose because it is common in varying amounts in body cells and tissues. It is the major component of the water molecule, which contains two atoms of hydrogen along with one atom of oxygen.

Scientists used their knowledge of nuclear magnetic resonance to study the molecular structure of various compounds, such as metals. Chemists and biochemists found it helpful for studying chemical structure and metabolic activity.

During the early 1950s, Erik Odeblad of Sweden suggested medical uses for nuclear magnetic resonance, which was shortened to NMR. By the 1970s, several groups of researchers in different countries were investigating its potential for imaging purposes. American physicist Raymond Damadian made key contributions. He studied the proton relaxation times in normal and cancerous tissues he obtained from experimental rats. He also noted variations in the magnetic resonance of tumors versus normal tissue. In 1972 American researcher Paul Lauterbur obtained the first NMR image. Scientists looked at a human chest in 1977 and, the next year, head scans were done on physician researchers who volunteered for the project. Then came some long-anticipated magnetic resonance images of the brain. In 1980 the technology was used to find a brain lesion.

Members of the Radiological Society of North America who attended that year's annual meeting in Chicago heard the exciting news about NMR. By then, it was ready for clinical use. Radiologists discussed the ways it might improve diagnostic medicine. They began referring to this technique as magnetic resonance imaging for fear that the word *nuclear* might provoke alarm or unnecessary safety concerns in patients.

The new technology appeared to be promising, but some questioned its potential risks. Unlike x-rays, fluoroscopy, and CT scans, MRI does not use ionizing radiation (gamma rays), so that particular aspect was not a health issue. However, since MRI uses large magnets to generate a magnetic field strong enough for the procedure, early researchers wondered how such a powerful magnetic field would affect the body. Could it harm the memory centers of the brain, for example, or damage eyesight? What strength magnet was safe to use? In the years since MRI was introduced, scientists have conducted safety studies, which over time revealed no harmful effects associated with the use of MRI.

During MRI, a magnetic field is generated around the patient inside the MRI unit. The nucleus of a hydrogen atom consists of a single proton. The magnetic field causes these hydrogen protons to line up. Then

PEERING ON THE INSIDE. MEDICAL IMAGING ALLOWS GLIMPSES OF THE BODY'S STRUCTURE AND INNER WORKINGS ONCE THOUGHT IMPOSSIBLE.

a brief burst of a radio frequency signal is transmitted. Radio waves of a certain frequency cause the protons to tilt slightly from their usually aligned formation. When the radio signal is turned off, the protons then resume their positions aligned with the magnetic field. The time between their being knocked out of position and then resuming their normal alignment is called the spin relaxation time. That process, regaining alignment, releases a small amount of energy in the form of a radio signal. It is these radio signals that make imaging possible.

Computers use this information to create a cross-sectional "slice" of the body. The computer, which must be able to process millions of bits of information quickly, detects and analyzes the currents. Then it assesses and measures the speed and volume with which the atoms return to their original positions. These measurements vary, depending on the type of body tissue involved. Areas with more protons generate stronger signals. The computer can then create a diagnostic image on the monitor. More detail can be obtained by adding other technology, for example by placing surface coils near the area of interest. Some tests also use contrast materials, administered intravenously, to enhance the images, which can be taken from different angles—front to back, cross-section, or side to side.

Like CT, magnetic resonance technology can produce three-dimensional images of the body on a screen. CT and MRI pictures may look similar, but MRI images will likely show more contrast among soft tissues. MRI goes beyond showing the structural details revealed in a CT scan to capture the physiological state of an organ. Because MRI examines atoms and molecules, the images reveal details about metabolic processes. This means that a physician need not wait for a tissue analysis to answer certain questions. MRI can show pathological changes in organs. For example, an MRI of the heart could show the difference between the muscle tissue and fat. It can also reveal the movements of the four heart chambers, the opening of cardiac arteries, and the volume of blood in the heart, among other details.

Researchers and physicians soon promoted MRI as an excellent way to diagnose tumors and study virtually any area of the body, especially the brain, spinal cord, heart, major blood vessels, musculo-skeletal system, and joints. An MRI can illuminate the details of a spinal disc injury that does not show up on a CT scan. It offers a useful means of diagnosing lung cancer because the images from MRI can distinguish cancerous tissue from the blood vessels found in the lungs. Just as important, this kind of imaging can help pediatricians diagnose conditions in children who are too young to describe their problem or to say what is ailing them.

Practitioners also found MR technology useful for imaging the brain. The gray matter of the brain is made up of 87 percent water, whereas the white matter is 72 percent water. Since MRI works on hydrogen atoms, it basically measures water, so these differences in brain tissue show up well on MRI images. Doctors have used MRI to monitor water movement in the brain and to spot chemical abnormalities and swelling, as well as detecting areas in the brain that are not receiving a normal amount of blood. This problem can occur with certain kinds of strokes, such as those caused by a clot, and early diagnosis can help to prevent further damage. Patients can receive medical treatments that reduce brain swelling and medications intended to prevent blood clots from forming and causing new strokes. If high blood pressure is an issue, medication and other treatments can be prescribed.

MRIs have proved effective in helping doctors to diagnose neurological problems, such as Alzheimer's disease and multiple sclerosis (MS), a disease in which the fatty insulating tissue around nerve fibers deteriorates and is covered with scar tissue, causing loss of muscle function and other problems. In a person with MS, the MRI scan reveals the scarring over abnormal fat-free areas on nerve cells.

By the time MRI was introduced, organ transplants had become part of standard medical practice. MRI scans are useful for monitoring transplant status. They may also be performed before transplant surgery in order to examine the blood vessels and other organs in the transplant area.

MRIs have been especially valuable in diagnosing brain tumors that did not show up in other tests. They can also help guide the neurosurgeon during the surgery to remove the growth. Sometimes neurosurgeons have to remove tumors that look just like the surrounding tissue.

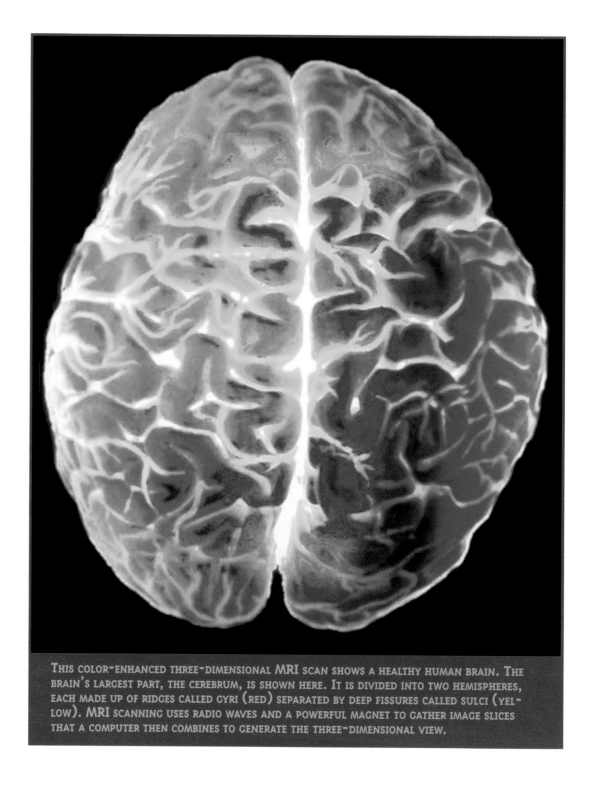

This color-enhanced three-dimensional MRI scan shows a healthy human brain. The brain's largest part, the cerebrum, is shown here. It is divided into two hemispheres, each made up of ridges called gyri (red) separated by deep fissures called sulci (yellow). MRI scanning uses radio waves and a powerful magnet to gather image slices that a computer then combines to generate the three-dimensional view.

In some cases, the surgeon may not even be able to see the tumor after making the incisions and looking at the brain itself. With brain surgery, it is crucial to remove all of the cancerous cells while avoiding all of the normal brain tissue. New technology can identify these opposing tissues much more clearly than was possible in previous decades.

An example of an MRI "success story" comes from author Howard Sochurek, writing in the January 1987 issue of *National Geographic* magazine: Nathan, a young boy, had experienced frightening and disabling symptoms that puzzled his physicians. From age two, he endured earaches and vomiting. Head pains developed at age five. He began to lose the use of one leg as well as the use of his left arm and hand. For several years, no cause was found. Then Nathan was given a CT scan, which showed a tumor in the medulla section of his brain. After doctors told his family that the tumor was inoperable, they sought other opinions and found a pediatric neurosurgeon who thought he could help. At Saint Joseph's Hospital and Medical Center in Phoenix, Arizona, Dr. Harold Rekate ordered an MRI. It showed a tumor near Nathan's brain stem about 1½ inches (3.8 centimeters) long, with a diameter of about ½ inch (1.27 centimeters). The next day, Rekate operated for more than eight hours. He was able to remove the tumor, leading to Nathan's full recovery. Commenting on the surgery, Rekate said, "Before MRI almost no one would have attempted it."

MRI does have its drawbacks, though. The equipment is expensive, costing several million dollars per unit. MR machines are costly to operate, too, since they require large amounts of electricity. The monthly power bill for an MRI can amount to several thousand dollars. MRIs also require more time than x-rays and other imaging procedures. MRIs cannot be performed on people who have a metallic implant, such as a cardiac pacemaker, in their body. The strong magnetic field turns metal objects, including keys and belt buckles, into dangerous flying objects, so they are banned from the screening room. The field can also erase the magnetic tape on a credit card. A small percentage of patients also cannot tolerate the idea of being enclosed in the machine during an MRI.

MRI technology continues to advance. Since the 1990s, most MRI scanners have featured a superconducting magnet, as opposed to the permanent or conventional electromagnetic types. They provide a uniform magnetic field that delivers superior quality images. Units containing these powerful magnets conduct electricity with no resistance, so very little power input is needed to maintain the magnetic field. They do require careful upkeep, however.

The 1990s brought additional new technology, including echo planar imaging (EPI) MRI. This technique allows for the early detection of strokes and may provide new information about the functions of different areas of the brain. New types of machines called open MRI were also designed that contain an opening so that the patient's entire body is not encased during the procedure. Partially open devices are regarded as more patient friendly and minimize the claustrophobia or anxiety some people experience during the procedure.

As of 2005 some new MRI devices featuring open-air superconducting magnets were available. They are cooled through electric refrigeration instead of liquid helium, which had to be used on the entire coil of the older superconducting magnets. In the future, scientists expect that MRI will play an even greater role in studying blood vessels and cardiac disorders. It may also be used to diagnose breast cancer. Examination of adjacent blood vessels also offers the hope of noticing breast and other types of cancer earlier, since the presence of cancer causes changes in blood vessels.

Scientists are exploring the possibility of using magnetic resonance to target molecules other than water. This development might help them to see details of metabolic processes in more tissues. They might study, for example, the metabolic action in muscle cells as the muscle contracts and relaxes. There may also be ways to target free radicals with magnetic resonance techniques. Free radicals are atoms or molecules having an unpaired electron. It is possible that free radicals may damage cells. Whether used alone or in conjunction with other imaging techniques, MRI continues to offer new possibilities for diagnosis and treatment.

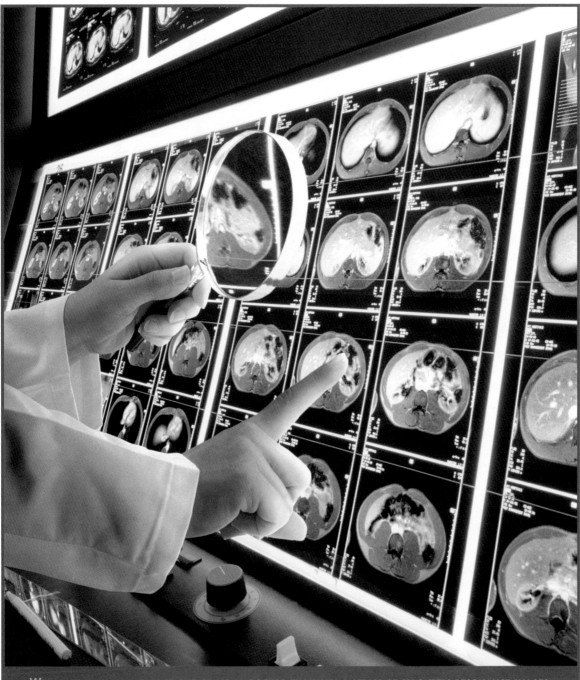

WITH THE HELP OF A MAGNIFYING GLASS, A DOCTOR EXAMINES A SERIES OF MAGNETIC RESONANCE IMAGES.

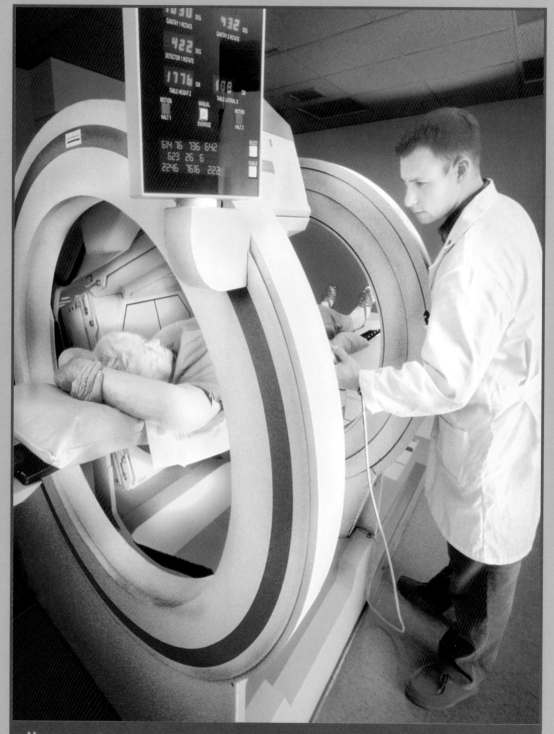

NUCLEAR MEDICINE IMAGING TECHNIQUES, EMPLOYING RADIOACTIVE ELEMENTS, GIVE DOCTORS YET AN-OTHER WAY OF LOOKING INSIDE THE HUMAN BODY IN A NONINVASIVE WAY. THE VARIOUS TECHNIQUES INCLUDE POSITRON EMISSION TOMOGRAPHY (PET), SINGLE PHOTON EMISSION COMPUTED TOMOGRAPHY (SPECT), BONE SCANNING, AND CARDIOVASCULAR IMAGING. NUCLEAR MEDICINE IMAGINING IS USE-FUL FOR DETECTING BLOOD CELL DISORDERS, INADEQUATE ORGAN FUNCTIONING SUCH AS THYROID DEFI-CIENCIES, IRREGULAR OR INADEQUATE BLOOD FLOW, ANEURYSMS, AND TUMORS.

Nuclear Medicine

Chest pain is a fairly common medical complaint. When a patient has unexplained chest pain, a doctor considers several possibilities. Does this pain result from coronary artery disease or a clot in the lung that is cutting off the blood supply? Are there signs of pneumonia? Performing a physical exam with a stethoscope and obtaining an electrocardiogram (EKG) as well as an x-ray of the chest may provide answers.

In some cases, the doctor schedules a myocardial perfusion scan, which is a type of procedure done in nuclear medicine. This test may be given when people have angina (unexplained chest pain that often occurs with exercise) or if they have an abnormal EKG. It allows doctors to look at the blood-flow patterns inside the heart. The images from a myocardial perfusion scan show where blood flow is normal and where blood is not circulating properly. Depending on the results, the doctor might order additional tests, such as a Doppler ultrasound image to check for blood clots in another part of the body, such as the legs. If clots are found, the doctor may prescribe medications, including blood-thinning drugs.

Nuclear medicine, also called radionuclide scanning, employs low-level radioactive compounds that help to provide images used for diagnosing and treating diseases. Radiation is used in this form of imaging, which can provide information about both the structure and functional state of organs. These images help health-care professionals assess physiological condition and track the path and spread of disease. The scans produced do not give the anatomic details of organs. Rather the images show an organ's shape and size and the way that it "takes up" the radioactive material. Another nuclear medicine technique called radioimmunassay can help to determine hormone levels or the amounts of therapeutic drugs in the body.

For a radionuclide scanning test, patients receive an injection that contains a radiopharmaceutical or the substance is administered orally. This solution contains special molecules or microscopic particles composed of a radioactive atom attached to a chemical that normally occurs in the body. Human cells can absorb these tagged molecules but do not metabolize them. The type of radioactive substance depends on the organ being examined. The radioactive substance or radioisotope must get to the correct place, which means that substances are target-specific. This process works because the body treats the radioactive atom and the normally occurring chemical in the same way. So the tagged isotope hitches a ride to the area being targeted. For example, when iodine enters the body, it goes only to the thyroid gland because the thyroid uses iodine to secrete a hormone called thyroxine.

When the patient has been administered the radiopharmaceutical, nuclear medicine cameras then image the photons (gamma rays) generated by the radioactive material. (In contrast, an x-ray machine creates photons that are then sent through a patient's body.) The image is produced as the machine detects the rays that emerge on the other side. Variations are detectable because different types of bodily tissues take up these chemicals at different rates. The amount of radioactivity the tissue absorbs and then emits can reveal its metabolic activity or its functioning on a cellular level. For example, some cells require more energy than others. Cancer cells absorb more radionuclides because they are rapidly dividing and multiplying. Infected bones are another example of tissues that use more energy than normal.

Nuclear medicine techniques have proved to be yet another boon for diagnostic medicine. The techniques are rooted in research that occurred soon after Roentgen encountered x-rays. One of the scientists who studied the mysterious rays was a French physicist named Antoine-Henri Becquerel (1852–1908). Becquerel's grandfather and father were prominent physicists who explored electrochemical phenomena and his father, Alexandre-Edmond, had discovered that some salts of uranium were highly phosphorescent—able to emit electromagnetic radiation both before and after being stimulated by a source of radiation.

Throughout 1896, Becquerel experimented with x-rays, using the chemical compounds and equipment his father had used to study phosphorescence and fluorescence. Early in 1896, he applied uranyl potassium sulfate to a photographic plate, which he covered with black paper and exposed to sunlight. When Becquerel developed the plates, he saw the image of uranium crystals. This phosphorescent substance evidently emitted radiation that could penetrate lightproof paper. Becquerel thought the uranium had absorbed energy from the sun and used that energy to emit x-rays.

Becquerel planned to expose additional uranium-covered plates to sunlight, but the February sky was cloudy. So Becquerel put the plates in a drawer and took them out a few days later. When he developed the plates without first exposing them to sunlight, he was surprised to see strong, clear images instead of the weak representations he was expecting. On its own, the uranium had emitted radiation. In 1899 Becquerel found that, unlike x-rays, the radiation from the uranium could be deflected by a magnetic field, because it consisted of charged particles. He had discovered natural radioactivity—the spontaneous emission of radiation, in the form of natural radionuclides.

The renowned Curies—Pierre (1859–1906) and Marie (1867–1934)—were conducting similar experiments. Marie Curie used the term *radioactivity* to refer to the phenomenon Becquerel described. While working with uranium ore, the Curies found some leftover elements in the ore that were even more radioactive than uranium. After four years of

AMONG FRENCH PHYSICIST HENRI BECQUEREL'S MANY CONTRIBUTIONS TO SCIENCE WERE HIS INVESTIGATION INTO WHETHER THERE WAS ANY CONNECTION BETWEEN X-RAYS AND NATURALLY OCCURRING PHOSPHORESCENCE.

painstaking work processing the ore and studying the material, Marie Curie identified two previously unknown elements, polonium and radium. Both elements were radioactive.

Becquerel and Marie and Pierre Curie each received a Nobel Prize in Physics in 1903 for their work on radioactivity. Marie Curie went on to receive another Nobel Prize, in chemistry, for her work with radium and polonium, making her the first person to receive two of the estemed awards. The Curie's daughter Irene continued her parents' work, with the help of the cyclotron, which American physicist Ernest O. Lawrence developed in 1931. The cyclotron uses magnetic fields to accelerate charged particles. Together these various developments paved the way for the use of radioactive materials in medicine.

At first, however, nuclear medicine involved treatment, not diagnosis. Radium was injected into certain cancerous tumors that could not be surgically removed. The discovery of nuclear fission during the 1930s brought changes. Scientists found that striking a uranium nucleus with a neutron could cause it to split into two new atomic nuclei. In the process, a great deal of energy was generated. After scientists found ways to produce a nuclear chain reaction, they were able to harness that energy for use in atomic weapons and for nuclear power. Other scientists also found certain radioactive by-products that occur during this process can be used in medical imaging.

Scientists learned more about artificial radionuclides in the 1940s, when radioactive iodine was used to treat cancer of the thyroid gland. Doctors found that the substance could also be used to detect thryroid disease and to show how effectively the thyroid was functioning. A rectilinear camera was employed to map the intake of the radionuclide. This type of camera, or scanner, could detect gamma rays and then communicate that data to a printing device that used dots to create an image. These images were recorded and used to assemble pictures of the organ's structure. Iodine-131 or iodine-123 is still used in diagnostic procedures to evaluate the thyroid. The rate at which the thyroid takes up the iodine-131 or -123 can be monitored with a scanning device to see if the gland is functioning properly.

THE FRENCH RADIATION PIONEERS PIERRE AND MARIE CURIE ARE PICTURED IN THEIR LABORATORY IN 1898.

Additional nuclear medicine studies were initiated during the 1950s. Researchers identified other low-level radioactive chemicals that could be introduced into the body and taken in by various organs. Better equipment contributed to the rapid growth of nuclear medicine during the 1960s. Gamma cameras, introduced in the 1950s, replaced the rectilinear scanner. The gamma camera (also called the Anger camera after its inventor Hal Anger) can detect and measure the faint signals emitted by radionuclides.

By the 1970s doctors were using nuclear medicine to produce images of more organs in the body, including the liver, spleen, and intestinal tract, as well as to locate tumors in the brain. Gamma rays cannot be focused, but computer technology has made it possible to see where the rays are coming from. Computers can process the information from the procedure and show a corresponding image on a monitor.

As time went on, researchers found more radioisotopes that were considered safe and effective for nuclear medical studies. Today, several dozen radioisotopes are in use. Technetium-99m is one of the most common. A form of sulfur can be used for studies of the liver, spleen, and bone marrow, while thallium is used to look at heart and other muscle tissues. Chromium, in the form of sodium chromate, attaches itself to hemoglobin, the oxygen-carrying molecule in red blood cells. As a result, chromium isotopes can help doctors observe how blood flows through the heart. Chromium can also be used to study diseases of the red blood cells, such as anemia.

Other radioactive isotopes are used to study the absorption of different nutrients in various parts of the body. These kinds of studies have shown scientists that certain organs may not receive vitamins, even though tests show high levels of these nutrients in the blood. For example, recent studies show that vitamin C may not penetrate the blood-brain barrier. Further studies are pointing out possible ways to deliver that vitamin to the brain tissue, since it can help counteract the effects of aging.

In the twenty-first century, nuclear medicine is making use of sophisticated cameras and computers. The development of faster computers, laser printers, and software has greatly enhanced these procedures. As of 2005, doctors could perform nearly one hundred different nuclear medicine procedures to obtain information about the major organ systems in the body. Most tests are being done to evaluate bones, the heart, or the lungs. Bone scans have shown doctors whether or not cancer cells have spread to a given area of the body. In the field of cardiology, nuclear medicine has helped people avoid certain invasive procedures, such as a catheterization. It enables doctors to evaluate the results of heart surgery or other cardiac procedures.

One of the most exciting forms of nuclear medical imaging is PETT (positron emission transaxial tomography), also known as PET (positron emission tomography). It was developed in the 1970s by chemists Michael Phelps and Edward Hoffman at the UCLA School of Medicine. The technology combines aspects of CT scanning with nuclear medicine techniques to reveal information about the body's chemical processes.

For a PET scan, the patient receives an injection containing positron-emitting radioactive atoms attached to chemicals like those normally found in the target organ, such as the heart or brain. After the blood delivers these chemicals, the radioactive atoms decay, emitting positrons. A ring of gamma ray detectors set up around the patient detects the resulting radiation. Then a computer integrates that information into a cross-sectional picture that shows the chemical activity that is occurring inside the organ.

PET has allowed scientists to observe the brain and measure its chemical activity better than previous techniques. What can neurologists see? Medical imaging techniques have not revealed a person's "thoughts," as sometimes happens in science fiction, but they are showing a great deal about brain function. The images reveal blood flow, chemical activity, and electrical signals. They also show what happens among the countless millions of connections inside the brain as people perform motor activities, make decisions, feel various emotions, and use their memory.

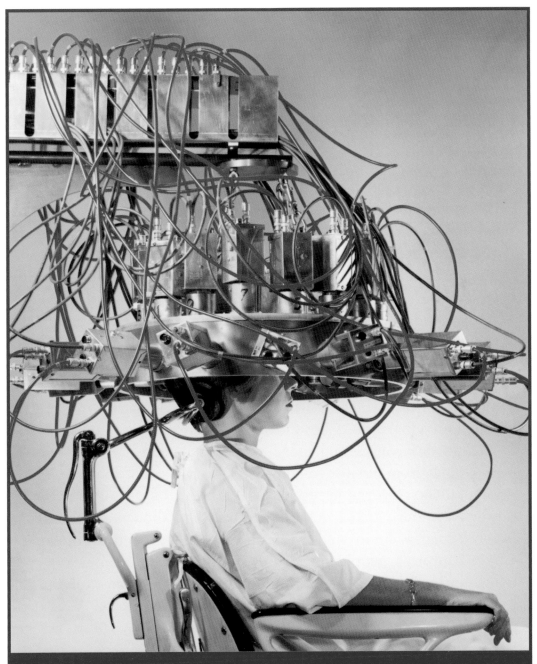

SCIENCE RESEMBLES SCIENCE FICTION WITH THIS MULTIDETECTOR POSITRON SCANNER USED IN CONJUNCTION WITH RADIOACTIVE SUBSTANCES TO HELP MEDICAL PROFESSIONALS LOCATE A TUMOR. PET SCANS DETECT GAMMA RAYS RELEASED WHEN A POSITRON OR POSITIVE ELECTRON FROM THE RADIOACTIVE SUBSTANCE INJECTED INTO THE PATIENT COMBINES WITH AN ELECTRON. SPECIAL SCANNERS DETECT THE RESULTING EMISSION OF RADIATION.

PET imaging of the brain has utilized a chemical with a structure similar to glucose (sugar), because the brain uses glucose for energy. After the patient receives radioactive glucose, various areas in the brain take it up according to their energy needs. This reveals the level of activity present in the different portions.

This kind of research has produced interesting and practical information. During the 1980s, scientists examined the brain functions of people while they looked at different scenes and patterns. They started with baseline readings while the subjects sat in a quiet darkened room. Then the people were told to look at paintings, trees, and other visuals. Researchers measured the amount of glucose used in the visual cortex to see changes as the subjects looked at objects with varying levels of complexity.

Other studies have shown how people use the different hemispheres of their brains (the right versus left side) for different tasks, such as listening to music. One study concluded that the visual centers in the brain come into play during listening as well as looking. These brain studies have also shown certain common brain patterns along with unique individual differences in the various responses detected.

Scientists have learned more about how brain patterns change as people move from infancy to adulthood. By the age of about 7½ months, the metabolic patterns in an infant's CT scan look about the same as those of an adult. Studies of brain anatomy also show the differences between teenagers' brains and the brains of people in their twenties.

For centuries, people have wondered how much of what we call "intelligence" is inherited. Does a certain type of brain determine intellectual potential? What does a high-functioning brain look like and what kind of biochemistry is involved? To answer these questions, scientists have analyzed the PET scans of people taking tests and compared these scans with their test scores. Studies show that people who score higher have brains that require less energy. In one study done in 1988, people who did poorly on certain tests used more energy in the cortical areas of the brain where abstract reasoning takes place. People with the highest scores used the least energy. Researchers concluded that the brains of people who demonstrate higher intelligence seem to be "organized" more efficiently. Researchers did not see differences in the brains' energy requirements when the subjects were asked to pay attention to flashing lights. A need for excessive amounts of energy may result from neurochemical imbalances, incomplete metabolism in the brain, or anatomical irregularities.

Some data leads to practical recommendations. Brain-imaging studies, combined with studies that follow people for years afterward, show the value of talking to babies and young children. Researchers have concluded that verbal stimulation at an early age will significantly affect future academic achievement.

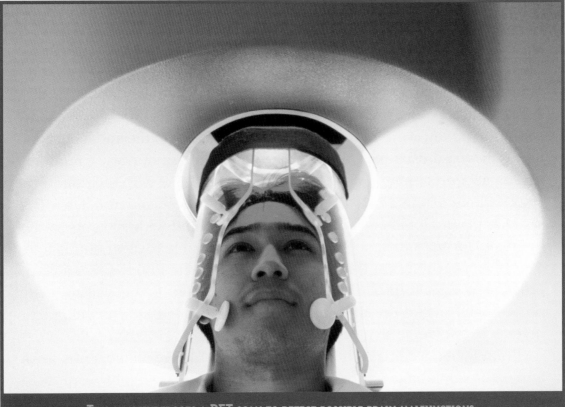

THIS MAN UNDERGOES A PET SCAN TO DETECT POSSIBLE BRAIN MALFUNCTIONS.

Besides normal brain functioning, PET can reveal disorders and diseases. Early detection is one goal. PET can help neurologists detect potential future problems in people who are still functioning normally. For example, from 1984 through 2000, UCLA researchers conducted a study of 284 people who had been experiencing minor memory problems. The PET images showed with 95 percent accuracy which of these people would develop dementia within the next three years. Other studies are being done to evaluate the effects of different drugs that might slow the progress of brain diseases and disorders. This kind of information can also help doctors who treat people with mental illnesses.

The brain images of people with different mental illnesses, such as schizophrenia and bipolar disorder, show distinctive patterns. Glucose usage in the brain is also lower among Alzheimer's patients and people with Down's syndrome than in people without any diagnosed neurological conditions. Alzheimer's disease can be detected with a PET scan. In an article for *Newsweek* in June 2002, Geoffrey Cowley wrote that Alzheimer's disease was once "diagnosed by exclusion. If you lagged significantly on a memory test—and your troubles couldn't be blamed on strokes, tumors or drug toxicity—you were given a tentative diagnosis and sent on your way. To find out for sure, you had to die and have your brain dissected by a pathologist." Now PET images of these brains reveal an accumulation of plaque in the areas that deal with memory. The places where plaque is present show signs of reduced activity. Scientists say that plaque builds up when certain fibrils bind with proteins in the brain and form a substance that the body is not able to clear out. Plaque displaces healthy brain tissue and, as a result, the brain is less able to produce acetylcholine, a neurotransmitter that is needed for the processes of cognition and memory. This neurotransmitter helps the brain cells exchange signals.

Brain imaging can also help show that psychiatric medications work for some people and not others. During the 1990s, studies were done with people who had been diagnosed with clinical depression but who did not respond to antidepressant medications. One study tested people

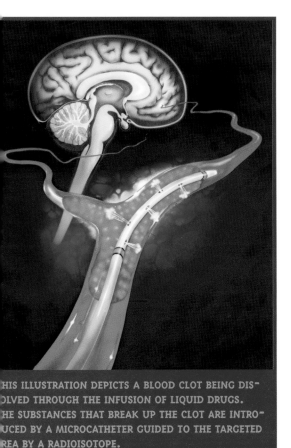

THIS ILLUSTRATION DEPICTS A BLOOD CLOT BEING DIS-
OLVED THROUGH THE INFUSION OF LIQUID DRUGS.
HE SUBSTANCES THAT BREAK UP THE CLOT ARE INTRO-
UCED BY A MICROCATHETER GUIDED TO THE TARGETED
REA BY A RADIOISOTOPE.

before treatment. The results showed that individuals who had lower than normal glucose metabolism in a part of the brain called the rostral anterior cingulate gyrus were most likely not to improve with antidepressant medication. The cingulate gyrus is one part of the limbic system, an area of the brain long thought to regulate emotions. The people with a higher than normal glucose metabolism rate in that same area were most likely to improve when on the same medication.

This kind of research could potentially help millions of people who suffer from psychiatric problems, in this case mood disorders. "These findings allow us to propose a critical role for this specific region of the brain in the complex brain network used to regulate normal and abnormal mood states," says Dr. Helen Mayberg, now professor of psychiatry and behavioral sciences at Emory University School of Medicine in Atlanta. "Our current thinking is that perhaps the rostral cingulate region serves as a critical bridge, linking pathways necessary for the normal integration of mood, motor, cognitive and vegetative (sleep, libido, motivation, appetite) behaviors, all of which are disturbed in patients with depression."

Dr. Mayberg is among those who think that such research can lead to better treatment and more effective ways of evaluating the impact of these treatments. She says, "[These findings] also point to the possibility of using PET results to help with diagnosis and management decisions for individual patients."

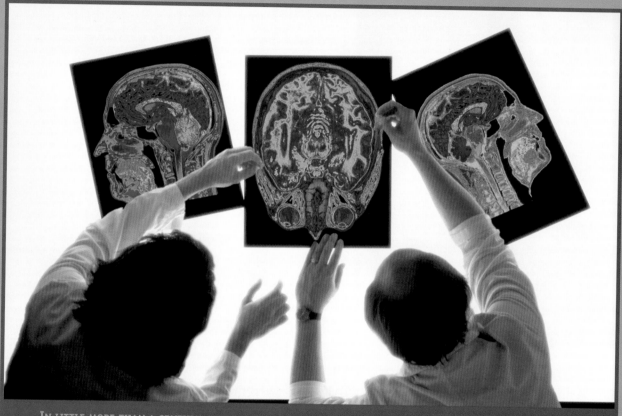

IN LITTLE MORE THAN A CENTURY, MEDICAL IMAGING HAS SEEN RAPID ADVANCEMENTS, GIVING DOCTORS A WIDER RANGE OF TOOLS AND PROCEDURES FOR TREATING PATIENTS.

Into the Future

In 2000 the American Roentgen Ray Society (ARRS) celebrated its one hundredth anniversary. Enormous changes had taken place since 1896, when Wilhelm Roentgen first saw the image of his bones on the x-ray screen. At recent meetings, members of the ARRS have discussed topics that reflect the ever-changing technology and applications in radiology, including the possibility of a virtual colonoscopy, using a limited CT scan of the abdomen in order to detect colon cancer; the use of high-resolution x-ray systems to help identify cases of infant abuse; the transmission of ultrasound images by telephone in order to diagnose people living in developing countries; and multidetector computed tomography (MDCT) to detect lumbar spine injuries that x-rays miss.

Medical imaging is increasingly in the news. Recent stories have profiled a variety of breakthroughs in the field and applications for new technology. Coverage has included discussion of PET scans that can help to differentiate between dementia caused by Alzheimer's disease and certain other conditions; an account of how doctors used information from CT and MRI to plan surgeries that would separate conjoined twins and build replacement parts the babies would need after being separated; new imaging techniques that guide the treatment of strokes in order to avoid extensive brain damage; a promising technique called magnetoencephalography (MEG) that might show which areas of the brain react to various types of stimulation, such as surprise; and brain-imaging studies that compare brain activity in fluent versus dyslexic readers.

Science magazine has called this era the "age of imaging." According to some experts, progress is occurring so rapidly that our knowledge could actually double every decade. Imaging techniques will be used to obtain the most useful functional, metabolic, and structural information for diagnosis and treatment.

New developments are occurring regularly in various types of imaging. For example, conventional x-ray systems are being upgraded to digital technology, which will eventually replace film cassette and film screen systems. As of 2004, digital x-ray technology was present in hundreds of locations around the world. It relies on phosphor plate technology, which traps x-ray energy. A process then releases the information that has been gathered and converts it into a digital picture. Digital radiography eliminates the need to store large films. As these changes take place, conventional x-ray film may eventually disappear.

In the area of ultrasound, four-dimensional devices are available. In another application, ultrasound transducers placed on the ends of probes allow doctors to conduct more thorough exams without surgery.

Doctors are finding more uses for a form of imaging called thermography. In this process, recorded infrared radiation produces images based on temperature differences in the body area. Recently, this technique has been used to investigate surface blood vessels and also tumors, since tumors register "hotter" than normal tissue. Osteoarthritis, on the other hand, is revealed in patches of cold as the disease progresses.

Another significant trend is the increasing use of more than one imaging modality to achieve optimal "views." Certain imaging techniques themselves use technology from more than one modality. One example is SPECT (single photon emission computed tomography), a form of imaging that emerged during the 1970s. SPECT combines nuclear medicine (involving the detection of high-energy photons) with x-rays and

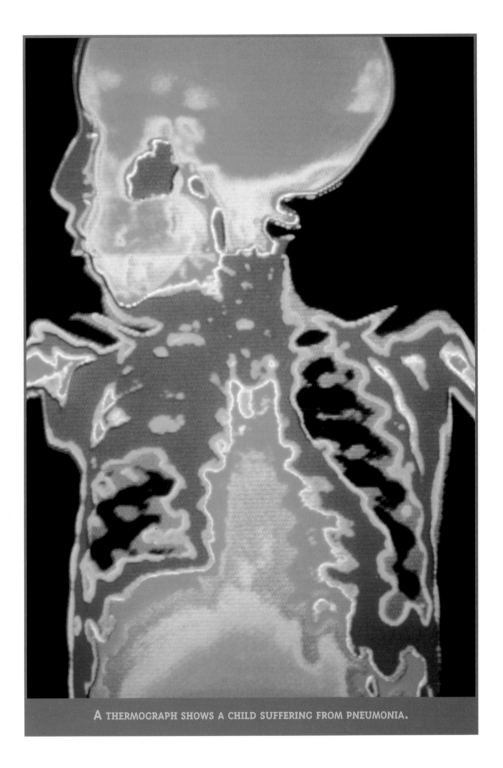

A THERMOGRAPH SHOWS A CHILD SUFFERING FROM PNEUMONIA.

CT. During the procedure, gamma imagers rotate around the patient to gather information from different angles. The resulting slice-images can be viewed individually or together in a three-dimensional picture, and from various angles. SPECT has been used to track blood flow in the heart and brain and to study brain functioning. The images that result can help explain problems with memory and show the differences between normal brains and those that have been damaged by drugs, such as cocaine or ecstasy.

SPECT technology and other imaging techniques may lead to more precise ways of determining the extent of brain injuries and predicting how much recovery is possible. This topic was highly publicized in 2005 when conflicts arose over the status of a woman who had been labeled "brain-dead." Forty-one-year-old Terri Schiavo had been in extended care facilities for more than ten years, kept alive with feeding tubes and other treatments. She had suffered severe brain damage when the blood flow to her brain was cut off for a period of time. Several neurologists claimed that Schiavo's CT scans showed atrophy and shrinkage of brain tissue. The scans showed that about 30 to 40 percent of her brain tissue had been replaced by water. Her EEGs (electrencephalograms) were "flat," supporting the conclusion that she was in a persistent vegetative state. Other people disagreed, calling the results inconclusive. They called for more tests, including PET scans and MRIs. The case sparked worldwide debates during a long court battle between Schiavo's parents and her husband. Florida courts eventually supported his petition to disconnect her feeding tube. Her parents disagreed, contending that their daughter showed signs of being able to communicate with them. They said they would care for their daughter if she was allowed to live. Nonetheless, the tube was disconnected in March 2005, and Schiavo died from dehydration and starvation.

More conclusive information about brain functioning in these cases may eventually be obtained by using radioactive tracers with advanced versions of PET and magnetic resonance spectroscopy, as well as brain electrical activity mapping (BEAM), a variant of the older EEG test, and techniques that have yet to be developed. New techniques for imaging the brain are helping neuroscientists make great progress in understanding the structure and function of the brain. Of course, more information would not necessarily resolve the moral debates that arise in cases like the one involving Terri Schiavo. As in other areas of medicine, new bioethical issues emerge along with changing technology.

What else does the future hold? Research is being done to develop "virtual reality" scanners. New forms of imaging may involve microscopic biological structures. These include scanned probe techniques and electrical impedance tomography. Nanotechnology promises to deliver smaller and

NANOTECHNOLOGY PROMISES NOVEL WAYS OF TREATING DISEASE. THIS COMPUTER-GENERATED ARTWORK PORTRAYS A NANOROBOT INJECTING A DRUG INTO AN INFECTED T CELL, A TYPE OF WHITE BLOOD CELL THAT FACILITATES THE CELLULAR RESPONSES OF THE IMMUNE SYSTEM. T CELLS CAN BE AFFECTED BY THE HUMAN IMMUNODEFICIENTY VIRUS (HIV), THE VIRUS THAT CAUSES ACQUIRED IMMUNODEFICIENCY SYNDROME (AIDS).

faster electronic devices and more detailed microscopic images of tissues at the cellular level. It offers the amazing potential to send microscopic sensors or other electromechanical devices into a part of the body, for example a blood vessel or parts of the GI tract. The sensor would obtain an image and transmit it. It might even perform a medical treatment, such as obtaining a tissue sample or performing a chemical analysis. In addition, microscopic deformable mirrors like those used in the most advanced optical telescopes are being mounted on computer chips. This technology will improve image correction.

Principles of immunofluorescence, a technique that is used to identify antibodies and antigens in blood samples, may be used in imaging. Antibodies, which are part of the immune system, are protein molecules. They could carry dye to various tissues and cells. Scientists would see where the antibodies attach. Based on the colors of the dyes, they could observe specific cell structures under certain wavelengths of light.

Scientists also expect to see more and more interdisciplinary collaboration. Medical imaging continues to benefit from developments in other fields relating to imaging and digital processing. One example is the technology used to explore outer space with satellites and cameras.

And just as computers and digital cameras have changed people's ideas about taking and storing photographs, this same technology affects medical imaging.

Change is occurring in the area of data collection and storage, as well as in sending, transmitting, and retrieving data. Teleradiology allows physicians to send CT, MRI, PET, and ultrasound images over telephone lines. Images can be stored electronically and recalled quickly and simply in various locations, as they are needed. Advances in computer technology will continue to affect medical imaging. Experts predict that we will eventually see the total digital operation of data and images.

Even the concept of the image has evolved. It is no longer considered to be just a pattern of lights and shadows on a piece of film. Imaging can be done with patterns of numbers stored in a computer database. People can then manipulate and display these patterns in different ways. They can work at three-dimensional imaging workstations in patient-care or in educational settings.

Using the computer to fuse different modalities will provide an even fuller picture of the body. Surgeons can "practice" their procedures ahead of time at a workstation, using the medical images that were gathered.

As well, the capacity to implement new developments in artificial intelligence and mathematical modeling can yield more information about a patient's condition without conducting further tests. This can minimize a patient's exposure to radiation, as well as save time and money. Imaging laboratories are developing these techniques, which are expected to become more commonplace in the years to come.

The use of computer-aided diagnosis—CAD—is also expected to grow. Using material from medical imaging and other sources, the computer can offer help with analysis, logic, and memory, all of which can enhance diagnosis and treatment. Nonetheless, health care professionals will continue to bring their experience, judgment, intuition, and common sense to this process.

High-tech companies continue to devote considerable resources to producing more sophisticated imaging equipment. Health care professionals will continue to face the challenge of choosing the modality that can produce the most useful information safely and efficiently at the least cost.

Radiology is a popular medical specialty. The people who work in medical imaging find that it is continually evolving, which makes their jobs both challenging and exciting. Some choose to work in specialized areas in the field, for example, neuroradiology or thoracic (chest) radiology, depending on their interests and skills. Dr. Harold G. Jacobson, who served as chairman of the Department of Radiology at Montefiore Medical Center in the Bronx, New York, said "A radiologist is constantly

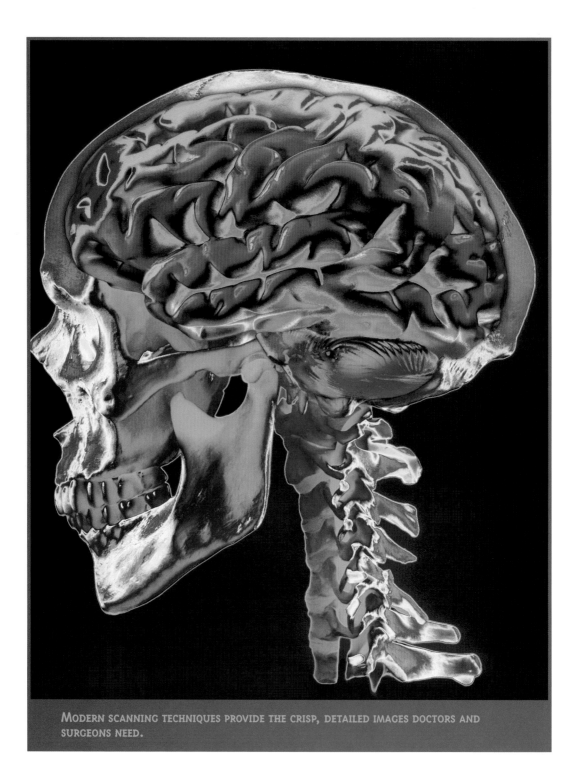

MODERN SCANNING TECHNIQUES PROVIDE THE CRISP, DETAILED IMAGES DOCTORS AND SURGEONS NEED.

dealing with challenges. You are 'Sherlock Holmes' trying to find the culprit by any means." Today's "medical detectives" have more tools at their disposal than ever before. The future promises even better imaging techniques that can be used in the unending effort to track down disease and promote better health.

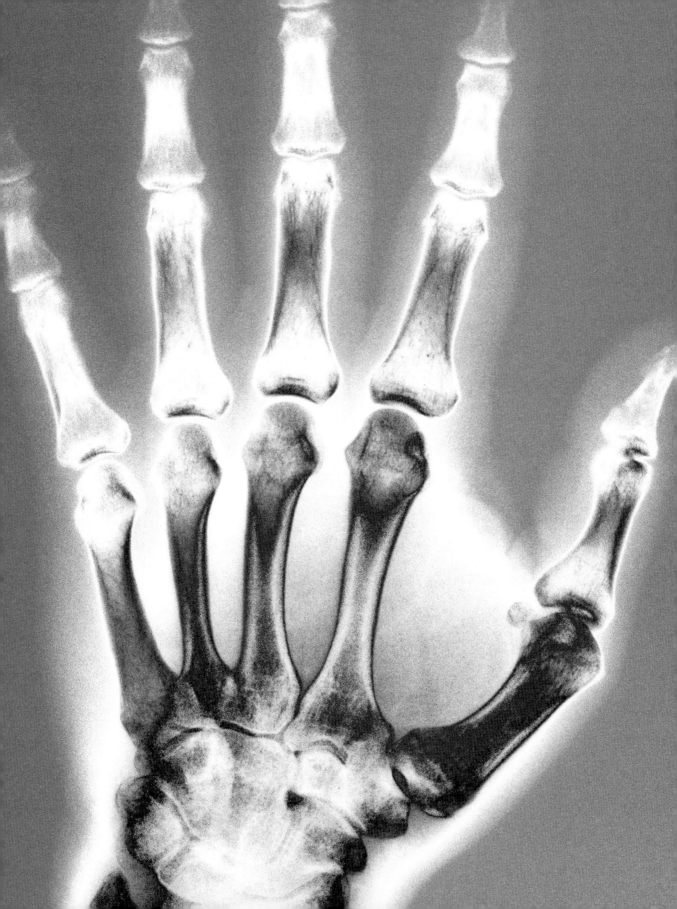

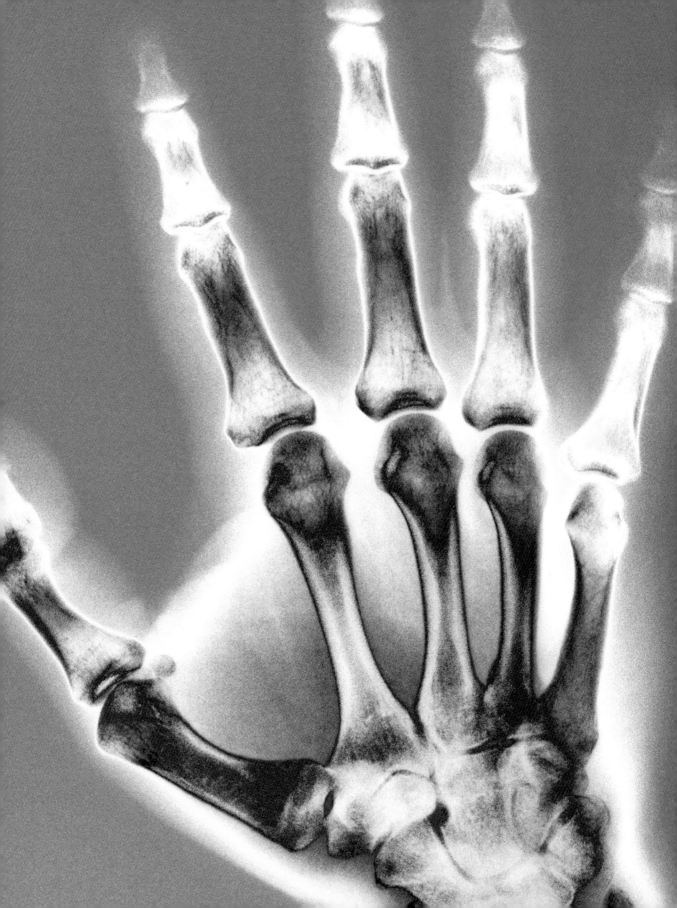

angiography—The imaging of blood vessels after first introducing a contrast agent that is opaque to x-rays.

anode—An electrode with a positive charge found in a storage battery or electron tube.

atom—The smallest chemical unit of an element; made up of a nucleus with a positive charge surrounded by negatively charged electrons.

cathode—An electrode with a negative charge found in a storage battery or electron tube.

chemistry—A branch of science that deals with the composition, structure, properties, and reactions of matter.

contrast agent—A material, opaque to x-rays, that is introduced into the body in order to generate images of body parts that would not otherwise show up; also contrast medium.

contrast imaging—The process of introducing a contrast agent to the body orally, through injection, or intravenously (through a vein) and then using x-rays or CT scanning to produce an image of the area.

cyclotron—A device used to accelerate subatomic particles to extremely high speeds along a spiral path using a fixed magnetic field and a variable electric field.

Doppler effect—A change in the observed frequency of sound waves or light waves that occurs when the source and observer are in motion in relation to each other.

electron—A very light subatomic particle with a negative charge (*See also* atom).

endoscope—A medical instrument that is used to view the inside of hollow organs, such as the intestinal tract.

fluorescence—The capacity of some materials to glow when they are absorbing radiation from a source.

fluoroscope—A device with a fluorescent screen that permits a continuous view inside the body while x-rays are aimed at the targeted area.

forensic medicine—The use of medical knowledge to resolve legal questions, such as those that arise in connection with crimes.

gamma ray—A form of electromagnetic radiation that has no mass and moves at the speed of light.

ions—A group of atoms that has become electrically charged by gaining or losing one or more electrons.

magnetic field—The condition that exists around a magnet or an electrical current.

molecule—The smallest unit of a substance that still contains its chemical and physical properties. It is made up of two or more like or different atoms.

mutation—An alteration in the cells of an organism that can be caused by exposure to radiation.

myelography—Imaging of the spinal cord and spinal nerves.

nano—Equivalent of one billionth; for example, one nanometer equals one billionth of a meter.

nanotechnology—A branch of science that uses materials and technology that can be measured in nanometers.

phosphorescence—Emission of light that follows exposure to a source of radiation and continues after that source is removed.

photon—An elementary particle of electromagnetic energy that can act as a particle or a wave.

physics—The study of matter and energy and the ways in which they interact.

pixel—Short for "picture element"; refers to a single point in a graphic image.

radioactivity—Spontaneous emission of radiation in the form of neutrons, alpha particles, beta particles, or gamma rays. This radiation occurs as a result of unstable atomic nuclei or a nuclear reaction.

radiograph—An image produced with x-rays.

radiologist—A physician who specializes in medical imaging tests and the use of radioactive substances for diagnosis and treatment.

skiagrapher—A person who specializes in taking x-rays and CT scans.

sonar—A system that uses transmitted and reflected sound waves to locate objects and measure distances between objects.

ultrasound—The use of ultrasonic waves for medical diagnosis or treatment purposes, for example for imaging internal body structures or a developing fetus.

x-ray—A high-energy photon or stream of photons with a very short wavelength.

1895
Wilhelm C. Roentgen observes and studies the phenomenon he calls x-rays and announces his discovery in late December.

1896
Henri Becquerel discovers radioactivity.
X-ray technology is used to image bones, teeth, and other parts of the body.
Thomas Edison develops his version of a hand-held fluoroscope.

1897
J. J. Thomson discovers the electron, showing that atoms are divisible.

1898
Marie Curie uses the term *radioactivity* to describe various kinds of radiations.
First military use of x-rays, by the British.

1901
Wilhelm C. Roentgen wins the Nobel Prize in Physics for his discovery of x-rays.

1904

X-ray researcher Clarence Dally dies, marking the first death blamed on long-term exposure to radiation.

1906

The first contrast x-ray image of kidneys is taken.

1910

The first contrast x-rays of the intestinal tract, using barium, are produced.

1912

Max von Laue shows that x-rays are a form of electromagnetic radiation.

1913

William Coolidge develops an improved version of the x-ray tube, made with tungsten.

1919

The first use of air injected into the spinal column as a means of x-raying the spine and brain (pneumoencephalography).

1927

Blood vessels are first imaged using a contrast agent (angiography).

1931

The National Committee on Radium Protection (NCRP) publishes its first safety recommendations.

1932

A spot-film device showing continuous series of fluoroscopic images is invented.

1940s

Nuclear medicine techniques using radioactive iodine to create images of the thyroid gland are developed.

1945
Images of the blood vessels in the heart (coronary arteries) are first produced using contrast agents.
Felix Bloch and Edward Purcell discover nuclear magnetic resonance.

1956
A major study showing a correlation between exposure to radiation and higher rates of leukemia and other cancers is released.

1957
Ultrasound is first used to produce an image of a fetus inside the womb.

1960
An endoscope is used to view structures in the gastrointestinal tract.

1962
Mammography to image breast tissue as a method of detecting tumors is developed.
The gamma camera replaces the rectilinear scanner for use in nuclear medicine studies.

1970s
The increased use of ultrasound imaging during pregnancy and development of Doppler ultrasound techniques for viewing blood vessels.

1972
Working independently, Godfrey Hounsfield and Allan Cormack develop CT scanning.
Paul Lauterbur obtains the first nuclear magnetic resonance (NMR) image.
Michael Phelps and Edward Hoffman develop PETT (positron emission transaxial tomography), which became widely used for imaging the brain.

1976
Robert Ledley develops "all-body" CAT scanning technology.

1979
Hounsfield and Cormack receive the Nobel Prize in Physiology or Medicine.

1980
Magnetic resonance (MR) is used to find a lesion inside the human brain.

1990s
MR scanners with superconducting magnets are developed.

2002
CT machines capable of collecting sixteen slices per scan are first used.

Center for Medical Image Science and Visualization
http://www.cmiv.liu.se

A Century of Radiology
http://www.xray.hmc.psu.edu/rci/centennial.html

RadiologyInfo
http://www.radiologyinfo.org/index.cfm?bhcp=1

A Short History of the Development of Ultrasound in Obstetrics and
Gynecology
http://www.ob-ultrasound.net/site_index.html

Society of Diagnostic Medical Sonography.
www.sdms.org

The Whole Brain Atlas
http://www.med.harvard.edu/AANLIB/home.html

FOR STUDENTS

Duin, Nancy, and Jenny Sutcliffe, eds. *A History of Medicine: From Prehistory to the Year 2000.* New York: Simon and Schuster, 1992.

Garcia, Kimberly. *Wilhelm Roentgen and the Discovery of X-rays.* Bear, DE: Mitchell Lane Publishers, 2003.

Hann, Judith. *How Science Works.* Pleasantville, NY: Reader's Digest Books, 1991.

Karolevitz, Robert F. *Doctors of the Old West: A Pictorial History of Medicine on the Frontier.* Seattle: Superior Publishing, 1967.

Kjelle, Marylou Morano. *Raymond Damadian and the Development of MRI.* Bear, DE: Mitchell Lane Publishers, 2002.

Murphy, Wendy B. and Jack Murphy. *Nuclear Medicine.* New York: Chelsea House, 1994.

Shorter, Edward. *The Health Century.* New York: Doubleday, 1987.

Sochurek, Howard. "Medicine's New Vision," *National Geographic,* January 1987, pp. 2–41.

FOR TEACHERS AND ADVANCED READERS

Cowley, Geoffrey. "The Disappearing Mind," *Newsweek,* June 24, 2002, p. 44.

Dakins, Deborah R., "CT Applications Expand Through Thick and Thin" Thin-slice CT 2004 http://www.diagnosticimaging.com/thinslicect/index.jhtml; jsessionid=OQ1KOS4OPP2XCQSNDBGCKHSCJUMEKJVN

Ester, Allen D., and Jonathan Burdette. *Questions and Answers in Magnetic Resonance Imaging.* Saint Louis: C.V. Mosby, 2001.

Gagliardi, Raymond A., and B. L. McClennan, eds. *A History of the Radiological Sciences: Diagnosis.* Reston, VA: Radiolog Centennial, Inc, 1996.

Gould, Paula. "The Rise and Rise of Medical Imaging." Physicsweb, August, 2003.

Kevles, Bettyann H. *Naked to the Bone: Medical Imaging in the Twentieth Century.* New Brunswick, NJ: Rutgers University Press, 1997.

Naff, Clay Farris, ed. *Medical Imaging.* San Diego: Greenhaven Press, 2006.

Rinck, Peter. *Magnetic Resonance in Medicine.* 5th ed. Blackwell Publishers, 2003.

Slone, Richard M., et. al. *Body CT: A Practical Approach.* New York: McGraw-Hill, Health Professions Division, 2000.

Page numbers for illustrations are in **boldface**.

About the Author

Victoria Sherrow holds BS and MS degrees from The Ohio State University. Her writing credits include more than sixty nonfiction books for young people, exploring such topics as biomedical ethics, health care, the First Amendment, and the Great Depression.